Mountains to Climb

I pledge allegiance to the flag
One Nation
Invisible.......
Faded Glory

by
Lester Wingate
Brother Gate

Mountains to Climb
Copyright © 2015 Lester Wingate
MasterWorks BookMakers Publishing Company

All rights reserved. No part of this book may be reproduced or transmitted in any form or by any means without written permission from the author.

ISBN (978-0-9833325-3-4)
Library of Congress Control Number (2015913215)

elijahblue_15@outlook.com
www.sankofastar.com

Dedication

I dedicate this book to every *"Veteran"* who responded with valor defending the ideas and principles woven into the fabric of our Nation. They are revered warriors with uncommon courage who sacrificed their lives defending the sacred promise of peace, security, prosperity and hope for a better future. Justifiably, they are our heroes; unselfish servants of humanity who *"sacrificed all for the sake of all"*.

For the multitude of Wounded Warriors still facing the daily battles of broken dreams, broken spirits, broken lives and broken promises; this book is offered as a conduit for hope and reclamation from the brokenness of war that has and continues to claim the lives of too many of our war stricken Combat Veterans.

The principles embedded in *"American Exceptionalism"* reflect an arrogance of our democracy which undeniable claimed the lives of 58,000 of our soldiers in Vietnam who sacrificed their lives in the trenches of ambiguity.

War is an ugly business and does not lend its power to forgetfulness neither does it easily release the tentacles of hopelessness and fear from a conscience laden with regret and suffering that seemingly never ends.

To my Hero
"Ralph"

Breathe

To my sisters Katherine, Joyce, Sharon and Angela and my brothers Air Force Veterans Francis and James
To Fran: *"I still am aspiring"*

Special thanks to Jennifer, Marlo and Betty for their unconditional support. A special appreciation to all the Brethren at Martinsburg, WV Hope Center who invested their trust in me; without them this would not be possible. To the VVA Chapter 1074 of Martinsburg, Tyrone and Mossie, thank you for carving out a path when there was none; a very inspiring example of what veterans can do working together. I particularly want to acknowledge my "Predecessors" who bore a torch of light; orchestrating my steps into the fold:

"Papa San Preston"

"Tony T"

"Willie the Professor"

To the Mayor, Isaac; thanks for the conversation that delivered me from wearing rose colored glasses. Thanks also for carrying my fears to the "Wall of the Dead" to face my greatest fear.

"Let this Voice be the Voice that Speak for Them"

Contents

Forward vii
Publishers Note xi
Authors Note xiii
Introduction xv
Riddle Man xix

Part One: Mountains to Climb

Chapter 1 Mountains to Climb 3
Chapter 2 Greetings 13
Chapter 3 Good Morning Vietnam 21
Chapter 4 The 60's Home and Abroad 39
Chapter 5 Agent Orange 57
Chapter 6 Agents of Rescue 69
Chapter 7 Fear 81

Part Two: Secret Battles

Sankofa 91
Kofi's View 92
Chapter 8 Coffins 101
Chapter 9 Be Careful 109
Chapter 10 No More Power to Weep 119
Chapter 11 Five Seconds to Midnight 127
Chapter 12 Amazing Grace 137
Chapter 13 The Caged Bird 153
Chapter 14 Door of No Return 161

Forward

"Mountains to Climb" is a must read for every veteran who served our country defending the ideas and principles embedded in our democracy. It is a probative exercise written with a unique perspective depicting the culture that existed during the Vietnam Conflict and the imperiling consequences so many veterans faced returning home to the unwelcomed streets of America. After 45 years of silence, out of reluctance I finally decided to move beyond the veil of years of denial and embrace the truth of a war that still bears its wounds. It was a two year journey bringing this book forward; a humbling ordeal not so easy when you consider the daunting task of accurately articulating my feelings of events that had such a devastating effect on my life.

Where others have written books, some archiving their day to day experience, I merely offer a summarization hopefully with a reasonable level of depth and transparency documenting my days in the "*Jungle*" and the impact the Social Revolution of the 60's played on the battlefield.

In this writing, I denote the changing paradigm of war and the institutions that propagate violence for causes other than freedom. With no degree of certainty to justify the perpetuated cause of our participation in Vietnam, the question remains in the conscience of a populous still riddled in doubt; "WHY"?

At the time of our deployment, the majority of our soldiers did not have an understanding of the history that preceded our involvement. It was imposed upon us as an act of duty never to be questioned. The Geneva Conference of 1954 had ended France's colonial presence in Vietnam and partitioned the country into two states at the 17th parallel pending unification on the basis of international supervised free elections. Ngo Dinh Diem was selected as Premier of the State of Vietnam and tried to settle the differences between the various armed militias in the South. Diem created a referendum in 1955 and declared himself President of the Republic of Vietnam (RVN). The United States provided military and economic aid to the RVN and sent U.S. advisors to assist in building the infrastructure. The Geneva Accord had promised elections to determine the government for a unified Vietnam. (wikipedia.org)

At the conclusion of our involvement, at best it can be said Vietnam was an aberration of success. As of today, the country has been normalized not because of our zealous endeavor to bring peace between the two rivaling factions but due to the striving will of a nation committed to resolve their *"own"* differences. As a result of our ambivalent policies, we saw the mass exit of millions of refugees fleeing for survival as a consequence of our failures. Vietnam remains as a lesson for those who would consider following our footsteps down the same beaten path that conspicuously claimed the lives of so many of America's dreams.

The Consequence of War

Vietnam still has its memories; some remain blurred as vapors dissipating in a smoked filled room while other recollections surface in the night as horrifying flashbacks of a battlefield of warriors who were engaged in the longest and most disputed war in American history. With the exception of our latest wars being waged in the Middle East, there is no other parallel to controversy surrounding deployment of our military than in the jungles of Vietnam.

War is the absence of peace. When the principles of peace are violated, struggles will emerge with laboring pains as a woman giving birth to a child. Whether it's political or economical, more often than not, the escalation of conflict arises from the simplest provocation; *"A contest of words!" "You throw stones at my house; I'll throw bricks at yours"*. The premise for resolving differences at times seems so ludicrous!

Words of emptiness spoken in opposition to the sacred values of others can become a breeding ground for contempt instigating retaliation and turmoil that can surface as a power infecting man's sensibilities. Liken to a dying man thirsting for water in a desert of drought, illusions began to surface from the privacy of his thoughts as a mirage of hope in defense of his beliefs. The perception of hopelessness derived from his insecurities will echo a battle cry as a drum beat to contemplating spirits deprived of respect and dignity. Divisive sounds of anger dissipating fumes of turbulence will stir to the boiling point of conflict. It then is just a matter of time.

*"Nobody is Hearing; Nobody is Listening;
Everything is Erupting"*

All men desire peace relative to their perception of *"Truth"*. When the patterns of their lives become fragmented, man and his quest for freedom and the *"Right to Be"* will explore every possibility to shape a reality reflective of his beliefs. This has gone on throughout the ages and will continue until our mortality ends.

War contaminates everything in its path at the cost of human sacrifices. It has consequences not so easily embraced when we truly consider the cost of its requirements. It's been said; *"Some gave some; Some gave all."* What a remarkable testament of those who only can be remembered. As pioneers of freedom, they have transformed the world to become a better place to live but yet the volatility of emerging cultures continues to challenge the establishment of order and civility.

Commonality in the shared domain of humanity emphasizes a need for peace, love, unity and respect for all of God's creation. There is no solution to war; *"It always has been and will always be; always one against another; the status quo resistant to change of something new."* Time is a constant with a measurement of intervals allocated for our choices. We can choose a life of peace eliminating the threat of war by our prudent decisions.

Publishers Note

MasterWorks BookMakers Publishing Company (MBPC) is based in the State of Maryland. With a proud tradition dating back to the inaugural of the new millennium, MasterWorks take pleasure in the presentation of creative authors who have contributed significantly to the categorical expansion of historical, inspirational and satirical writings. The relevancy of their publications archived in our library is indicative of ambitious and creative minds. They will excite your passion challenging you to *"Dig a Little Deeper"*.

> *"When our choices are reconciled with those who are willing to apprehend the mantle of peace, dialogue will replace weapons of fire; respect will give credence to difference; and love will silence the voices of hatred that fumes in the hearts of adversarial persuasions."*

Authors Note

Writing is a sequestered journey navigating through the channels of our imagination. It is a captivating experience; a search for an expression of life that can only be captured in the power of our words. It has a freedom to examine our introspections and display them as an articulation of our imaginings. The visualizations flow as a river exuding with passion at the center of our existence. They reveal the imprint of our experiences, a collection of our dreams, hopes and visions reflective of the patterns framed in our imagination.

In these sequestered moments, there is a reverence preserving the treasures of our innermost feelings. When our thoughts connect with our passion, a power emerges capturing our world of imagination and frames our conscience to reflect the reality in which we live. What was once hidden, buried deep in the secrecy of our inner chambers, now unfolds as our perceptions of truth.

Introduction

I have spent years of my life sequestered with memories of Vietnam. It was a life of seclusion; entangled in a spider's web of introspection with haunting recollections not so easy to forget. Introspection is hiding; a retreat into an inner life veiled in secrecy purpose to resolve deep rooted challenges that frequently clutter our paths. Introspection provides insight through self examination of our thoughts, feelings and motivations so often circumvented by our decisions of denial.

It wasn't necessarily by choice I entered into a manic state of separation but as a consequence of lost enthusiasm resulting from bridled emotional trauma. Cumulative years of unresolved issues dating back to the turmoil of the *"Jungle"* left an irrevocable imprint embedded deep in my psyche. In an atmosphere filled with unimaginable desperation, the chaotic culture of Vietnam will forever be a lasting memory.

Prose

Attributes of the human experience are consistent in the lives of all God's humanity but our trials take a unique path relative to our life's experiences. Despite our uniqueness, there is commonality in our joys, sufferings and even our tears. What's prevalent in your life today is indicative of a path we all must consider. Some are being born while some are dying; some are laughing while others are crying; some are mending while others are hurting; some are praying while others are void of believing; some are sharing while others are not even caring.

Throughout this writing, the abstract of my feelings are captured in prose. Prose is an expression that may be foreign to some but thought provoking to others. It is quite difficult to accurately articulate a transparent measurement of one's pain and suffering that is coherent to others. Insecurities resultant from years of inward denial and agonizing frustration of *"issues of the heart"* requires a conscientious ear of others to accurately respond to abstractions embedded so deep in the heart and soul of a person. It's like a cloud that refuses to rain but given time will release itself just as a flood gate is overwhelmed by a racing river.

What's been hidden; buried beneath years of layering is a place of discovery that can only be captured in the privacy of prose. It reveals the reflection of the heart that can't be described in any other way. It penetrates deeper, closer to the heart than mere words and is written as an expression of our deepest affections.

Prose is an abstract; as abstract as a Picasso painting blurred in an enigma of interpretation. The collection of our thoughts and feelings will portray as a mosaic reflective of our character and integrity developed over time and seasons. Seemingly, prose does not always have a rhyme of time and seasons, but it does reflect the poetic justice of the trials of living waiting for a verdict worthy of a legacy relative to our investment.

A Challenging Path

We can no longer afford the compromise of neutrality at such a critical hour with the clock still ticking beyond our ability to recover. It is significant we leave a legacy that will bring honor and recognition to those who have paid such a dear price for the honor to serve our Nation.

It is my hope in this writing that you will be challenged beyond the point of where your understanding is settled and examine the passion at the core of your existence. As a dialogue of truth, I trust it will lead you down the path of enlightenment to excite the investment of God's gifts we are so reluctant to apprehend. As we take this journey through the tributaries that give passage into our inward treasures; *"The secret fires; guarded places only trusted to ourselves";* we are to be reminded of the sacrificial offerings of those laid at the altar beneath a flag stained in blood.

Regardless of the depth of our sufferings and misgivings, we must confront the source of our fears and those who have misrepresented our legacy. We've been made into an outlier in comparison to any other Veteran of Foreign Wars who participated defending the promise of our Nation. The time has come and *"it is now"* to cease the dialogue of excuses which only creates more diverging opinions.

"Riddle Man"

I will go to that *"Mountain"*
while the day breathes its last breath, and the shadows run away.
Come with me from the peak of the
"Snow Mountain"
from the lion's caves, from the *"Mountain"* of the leopards,
where there is a fountain of fresh water
flowing down from the *"Mountains"*.

King Solomon (14)

Riddles are designed to excite our imagination. They speak metaphorically as a flame of light exposing what's hidden from our sight. A riddle's conclusion rest in the eyes of the beholder; *"The way you view it is the way you do it"*. Riddles are quite intriguing and thought provoking which requires digging a little deeper well below the surface to resolve their underlying meaning.

As a child I read the riddles of Solomon trying to make sense of the patterns that were far beyond my ability to comprehend. They were very poetic and fascinating to say the least. Consequently, I began to write my own riddles, parlaying with words in a poetic stream of new found enlightenment. With the breath of my conscious exhaling in passion as fast as a cheetah's heartbeat when he finds his prey; the panting of my imagination began to flourish.

My youth was full of dreams; dreams that captured my imagination of a world full of possibilities. I often reminisced at night looking into the heavens at shooting stars flying by. Those same shooting stars reappeared in the killing fields of Vietnam. It took me back to the days of innocence when I would lie on the ground with my eyes roaming from one end of the sky to the other. I often contemplated; *"Why do shooting stars only come out at night?"* It was rather amazing to discover that the combined strength of all the stars gave way to the blinding light of the sun which overshadowed everything in its surroundings. The universe has its secrets; some revealed by the light of day and others hidden by the darkness of night. Time and eternity are one in the same. There is no difference between day and night. They are the same day; same challenges carried from one day to the next.

While searching the canopy of the darkened sky, I tried to transpose the coded message of twinkling stars pulsating in sequence, blinking as if to draw my attention away from the confines of gravity to escape to an unknown land. I waited for chariots to arrive but they never came; left only to believe in Santa with reindeer flying through the sky. I searched endlessly from one star to the next looking for answers; *"Where did all this come from; where did all this begin"?*

With my thoughts racing as I searched deep into the heavens looking for the beginning of my beginnings, there was no end in sight. While enraptured with reflections of something bigger than me, I imagined that my travels began as the travel of a falling star in search of a landing. Just as shooting stars fall from heaven to earth sparkling with light, I passed through the cosmic prism of time landing upon the grounds of Earth which had been waiting for my arrival. With blaring trumpets as angels serenading in a melody of music from centuries past, I made my landing for a journey on a road filled with uncertainties. With a bang like the intensity of a comet's fire dissipating in a vibration of colors, the purity of light that existed from the beginning of my travels separated into a chromatic imprint of my existence; from the reflecting colors of jasper to a martyr's bloodstone of jade and transparency of the purest diamond. The color of my vessel was an earth tone of brown clothed in a garment stitched in black. It would be a garment that would bear shame, suffering and pain but more significantly it would be; "*A Garment of Darkness Most Appealing to the Light*".

    I still miss those precious days of my innocent beginnings. The captured fragrance of garlands and the aroma of pollinated wild flowers enraptured in a gentle breeze as they raced across fields blooming with nectar still linger in the corridors of my mind. I can still hear the songbirds singing in celebrated unity and the static flight of the hummingbird's wings beating against the wind. The silent beauty of the butterfly arrayed in colors of splendor extracting honey from those delicate blossoms of *"Honeysuckle"* petals was a remembrance of spring.

From Profundity to Truth

"The Light of Truth" is a light that searches the heart of every human being. From our day of beginnings, it shines as vibrant rays emanating from the sun only to flicker as a candle struggling to survive in the twilight of a dimensioning future. It has no definition other than *"Truth"* itself and is personified as an exhibition of the life we live.

However provoking my thoughts are captured; this book in part is intended to be a source of inspiration as well as an instigator of truth; bringing clarity to issues maligned in controversy that as of today, still continues to besiege an unsympathetic generation who disavowed our legacy and never accepted our service with any degree of validation.

We are made better by the wisdom of our history learning from our mistakes and failures as we advance toward a more noble cause of bringing peace, justice and the acknowledgment of truth to our humanity.

"Be true to yourself." Every word released into the atmosphere is attached with energy. They have power to frame the visions of life; from broken dreams into a blueprint of restoration for all of our gifts and talents.

> *"If a man does not keep pace with his companions, perhaps it is because he hears a different drummer. Let him step to the music which he hears, however measured or far away."*
> Henry David Thoreau

Part I

Mountains to Climb
"Hidden Places"

Spitfire

Someone that's wild & free, & that can say what he/she wants to say without a care in the world. Also, someone whose angry words sting like fire....
"Urbandictionary.com"

Chapter 1

The first U.S. casualty in Vietnam was Flying Tiger John T. Donovan who was killed on May 12, 1942, but American involvement in Vietnam was not considered official at that time and as such his name does not appear on the Vietnam Veterans Memorial. (1)

Mountains in all their beauty are fixed in time. They exist as a chronology of the competing forces of nature evidenced in their rugged stature. On one of my weekly trips to the meetings with the Combat Veterans at the Hope Center in Martinsburg, West Virginia, I became fixated on the rolling hills, peaks and valleys of the mountainous range of West Virginia's Shenandoah Valley. It was so majestic! I marveled at the awesome display of the turning leaves of autumn that blanketed the landscape. What a remarkable exhibition of colors reflecting in brilliancy through the prism of the sun's rays and the breathtaking view of the multi-layered shades of the colors of life. A new sense of freshness filled the air temporarily liberating constraints on my imagination. This was truly an awe-inspiring moment that instigated reflections of days gone by.

The manifestation of God's beauty and awesome display of His majesty was in contrast to the tears that began to flow from years of unresolved turmoil that was ravishing my conscience. The ending of one season going into the next always has its moments of expectation but this was to be no different with the added disappointment of another year I couldn't reclaim.

As I peered into the endless blue sky searching for a canopy to hide my tears, the feeling of sorrow began to permeate within my vacillating emotions of memories past. *"It was the memory of War."* You will never outrun your tears. Those salty drippings of despair will come and go when you least expect.

There are times the fleeting moments of comfort comes as a hopeful embrace of relief but the reminders are still there of the unforgettable sounds of men dying; men crying; men hurting and men who stop believing. Smells, sounds come as a bombardment of rushing waves of fear. We've come to know this as PTSD. After years of struggling to maintain the ordering of our lives, the struggle still continues.

At best, it can be said that war is an interrupter. It stands between the youthfulness of yesterday's dreams and the hope of rearranging the shattered fragments that were so dispersed in confusion. Repercussions stemming from my participation in Vietnam are traceable to events created on the battlefield. I entered the war secured in my identity but as a consequence of my involvement, I returned home with my life in shambles beyond recognition of my former self. The most impressionable years in my development of becoming a man were given to a cause that bears no significance to the life I am now living. The gains are unrecognizable as they have produced a myriad of circumstances that continue to deliver obstructions in my daily life.

As I continued my morning drive sequestered in a surreal moment of thought while peering at the surrounding elevations, I considered; *"Where are the birth place of mountains? Where did the mountains in my life originate?"* While pondering for answers, I felt a provocation stirring in my emotions.

The fervor of my inflections began to rise to the surface and I was forced to deal with a truth beyond my denial. I realized that mountains had become my hiding place; a place where my emotions were masked behind an impenetrable granite of stone. What you saw on the outside was a facade of what was buried so deep within me. It was a well protected place fortified with a vault of memories layered over time.

As years would come and go, the accumulated power of an emotional volcano's eruption would shift its balance within me causing a seismic flow of tears burning with fire as the mantle of grace upon my life continued to lose its luster. At the peak of turmoil brewing beneath the depths of my confusion, the volatile eruption of fiery explosions relieved its pressure and began to flow as a river of destruction, destroying everything that was in my path. Mountains can harbor destruction but some lie in passivity, silenced in power as a testimony sealed in time waiting for an impulse to trigger devastating events in our lives.

Seasons change; from summer's sabbatical to the covering of snow and ice in winter's mix of emotions as an elicit call for hibernation; standing alone surrounded by an atmosphere resistant to light. Inwardly we search only to find a *"Man in the Mirror"* waiting with the reflection of memories that has shaped our lives. It provides us with the opportunity to *"be true to ourselves"*; away from the voices and opinions of others. Being transparent, we will find ourselves stripped of our own deception; left with a liability only we can own.

Birthplace of Mountains

The Earth is a collection of towering mountains filled with oceans and plains for our dwelling. In the canyons of the deep and valleys carved out of time, streams of living water rest beneath the towering presence of monuments rising high into the clouds. Refreshing springs seeping from their base flow in effervescence giving life to all its inhabitants as shallow brooks mirror the reflection of life above.

As Combat Veterans, we've structured our lives as a towering mountain elevated into peaks unknown; too high for others to climb and seemingly, too low for heaven to reach us. But yet the compassion of our tears falling at the base of our contentious emotions forms as a swirling pond in an entrapment of fear while we search through our darken memories to connect to a tranquil moment of peace. With our peaks high into the clouds, our tears are always refreshed as it continues to rain upon our despair. For those below resting beneath our protective wings, falling rain is refreshing as water falling upon a pad of lilies in the bloom of spring. But high above, life continues to vaporize as tears of pain. Moans of thunder can be heard echoing through the air as clouds of despair continue to descend upon us. As a bombardment of missiles targeting its prey, flashing lightning scorches the ground as we cry out in agonizing captivity, reverberating in our struggle to be free. Everybody below runs for cover until the silence of our pain returns settling their fears.

Take a look at the intimidating elevations surfacing from the earth in their towering glory and you will discover they are only limited by the boundaries of the firmament. Only the heavenly bodies of the sun, moon and stars in the infinite domain of time are raised higher than their peaks. Mountains did not suddenly appear. They existed before becoming visible covered in obscurity in a sea of circumstances.

Brooding deep in the hidden chambers of the ocean, well below the surface, mountains only gave evidence of their existence by a pillar of smoke erupting through the air. As the eruptions continued cool sedating water turned the lava into hardened molten. The bigger the eruption, the more replenished their mantle became causing them to rise higher in stature from the depth below. By the time they became visible, they had already created a life of their own; an island surrounded by water; separated and isolated, trapped with nowhere to go. The settling moments of pacification by the chilling waters of the deep only served as a temporary retreat from the turmoil that continued to brood beneath the surface.

The formation of mountains is a very violent process, always *"feeding upon itself"* until it reaches its destructive limits. As long as it is active, it has the potential of transforming into a *"volcano"*, erupting with liquid streams of fire flowing from depths unseen.

Invisible Mountains

The construct of mountain formations is indicative of the havoc that exists in the life of most Vietnam combat veterans. Our lives have the same reverberating internal turmoil as an unstable mountain that has resonated for the greater part of our lives; a 50 year reflection of time never to be reclaimed. The eruptive effects are the same with the difference being mountains don't move but the circumstances of our lives are ever so transient, spewing as a destructive flow of lava racing down a hill in search of an ending.

The daily volcanic eruptions formed over years in the deep waters of disparity forms as irrevocable memories perpetuating the hardening of our hearts. Only when the ash of debris from violent erupting geysers of our pinned up emotions is cleared away can the source of help freely flow. There is a path open to us but we must choose it and follow the prescription given to mitigate the stirring of unrest that refuses to cease.

On the surface of our defeated elevations, waterfalls are formed. The waterfalls flowing from within are the silent weeping of inward turmoil surfacing as tears that continue to flow from our *"mantle of weeping"*. They drain away the sediments of despair to reduce the pressure to keep us from tumbling into further despondency.

The cool sedating waters of forgetfulness at times have a pacifying effect but eventually will wear off and the problems are still there; erupting with greater intensity than before. It then becomes a challenging diagnostic adventure to comprehensively analyze our issues still masked behind a shield of misery and suffering.

What we carry around on the inside fully camouflaged in fatigues of pain will remain undisclosed until it reaches that monumental level of no return; *"Visibility"*. What was born in secrecy has now become visible to everyone. The emergence of the problem is now standing tall and transparent for the world to see. We cannot hide it any longer!

As years have gone by, quicker than the youthfulness of our dreams, our memories of those dreadful war stricken days are etched in stone as a testament of a life we once lived. Wars are not constant. The unpredictable nature of human beings in their evolving struggles of the *"Right to Be"* dictates that at some undefined milestone, inevitably, conflict will arise in defense of the values unique to their development.

Chapter 2

Greetings

The concept of war dictates a never-ending truth of its brutality; *"Kill or be killed; Live or die!"* Every war has its limitations framed by an ideology by those seated in power who determine how our wars will be waged. The rules of engagement can be frustrating adhering to a set of principles not conducive for those who actually commit their lives without consideration of the consequences.

Our Politicians more likely than not often speak without the voice of courage to defend their rhetoric and at the same time will do everything in their power to protect their love ones from the error of their judgment. The legacy of the Vietnam era was an *"Era of Deferments"*; a new criterion for unwilling participants who sought deferments as a means of escaping such an unpopular war. The rich and privileged of this country will never take ownership of a war for fear of the ultimate sacrifice. It's always someone else's battle; those naive of the power of war and its lasting consequences.

It seems rather ludicrous to have our principles debated by committees sequestered behind closed doors who are clueless and arrogant in their assessment of the expense of war. Every war has its own agenda; a clear accountability of its cause, purpose and discretionary judgment delegated to the men and women who put themselves in harm's way assuming a risk of uncertainties.

When decisions are made by the powers that be to commit the lives of our citizens to war, exposing them to atrocities, every consideration must be given for the sacrifices required. Without a probable cause as being the case in our most recent Iraq War, it is my opinion, the decisions made to engage in war reflected dereliction of responsibility of not having learnt from the mistakes of our involvement in Vietnam. More lives; more blood; youthful dreams scattered in the non-returning winds of time.

If you were to ask anyone today of our defining mission in Vietnam, there would be a variety of opinions. Absent the declaration of a mission of why were we sent to such a dreadful place has frustrated a vast number of Vietnam Veterans in their quandary for validation. *"Why were we there and what were the benchmarks to be accomplished? What were our guiding principles that would foster success?* What started as a crisis never turned into a war but yet 58,000 souls lost their lives for no justifiable reason. So many were in the prime of their lives; babies fighting a nonsensical grown man's battle that could have been settled from its beginning at the negotiating table of diplomacy.

Was it to combat Communism, Ho Chi Minh, save the Vietnamese from themselves or promote the cause of greedy *"Politicians"* whose only interest was financial gain exceeding the value of the human lives they were sacrificing? Besides the fact of surviving, there is no justifiable reason I can give for participating in what I deem as *"crimes against life"* perpetrated against another human being.

"Greetings"

Intellectually, I was too young to embrace the concept of war and conviction required to be a soldier but instead held true to my aspirational dreams of completing my education without the unwanted interruption of being drafted. At the time of my entry into Vietnam, I was an immature teenager of 19 years. The concept that I could die during my tenure in a land so far away from home was most humbling and very difficult to grasp. It seemed so unreal and contrary to any truth I gleaned from the sphere of influences surrounding my childhood. From the time of those youthful days of naiveté to that dreadful day of opening my personalized *"Draft Letter"* from Uncle Sam; up until then I did not lend any significance to my name. But the U.S. Government was quick to inform me just how special I was; *"Greetings"*! After reading such a welcoming salutation then bam; "What the..........."!

Initially, I was very reluctant to accept Uncle Sam's offer but realizing the severity of the consequences of refusing, better judgment prevailed. I had not yet completed my first year of college and was not ready to be thrust into the responsibility of manhood so soon. I was pursuing the passion of my dreams of becoming *"who I wanted to be"* and never considered the possibility of dying in the sweltering heat of a jungle mired in conflict!

The nightly news coverage with Walter Cronkite fed into my paranoia as the daily count of our young men saw the tragic end of a life they were just beginning. We never gave them a chance; could have but we didn't; should have but we still didn't! Perhaps my reluctance to enter the war was not necessarily because my individual choices were infringed upon but because of fear of being the next statistic of Cronkite's reporting.

It was a challenge to adjust my thinking to accommodate the idea of becoming a soldier when it never was part of my consideration from the beginning. This was as unwelcomed as an Achilles' heel; a slow death thrashing with self-inflicted anguish of submission to do something against my will. Ultimately, I made the decision to comply with our government's request which eliminated the continual threat of imprisonment or revoked privileges as an American citizen which was a price I was not willing to pay.

As I reflect on Muhammad Ali's (Cassius Clay) refusal of being drafted, I marvel how times have changed from being yesterday's villain to become a beloved son now turned America's hero. He has gotten more respect by taking on the system as a *"Conscientious Objector"* in his refusal to comply than the years of obedience I suffered as a consequence of my participation in a cause I vehemently rejected. I am not envious of him; I respect him highly not so much as a prize fighter but as a man who became more principled in his convictions regardless of what it would cost him.

Time is the most precious commodity we have and the importance we lend to it should be reflective of the values and choices of our individuality. However, I do believe in exceptions. As an American, in times of conflict and wars in defense of our democracy, it is incumbent upon us to answer the call for our service. It is not left up to us to pick and choose a war suitable to our expectations.

In a country with so many beliefs and faiths, it should be noted, as a Nation we stand for the principles written in our constitution and not religion that fuels our ideology. The ideology of religion dictates that anyone for any reason can disqualify themselves based on their beliefs at the burden of others to substitute for their denial. The lines of demarcation between *"Church and State"* have been clearly defined dating back centuries upon the founding of this democracy. For that reason, I rejected the anarchical tendencies that had flooded my conscience and chose the path of compliancy. Without any other consideration, it was the path of least resistance toward continuation of fulfilling my dreams.

Today's military is strictly voluntary. As a result of lessons learnt from Vietnam, America's appetite to maintain a draft pool of eligible candidates to increase our military strength in a time of war has been rejected and substituted by a new unsuspecting draftee; *"The National Guard"*. Their primary function provides the necessary reserve for our state and federal government. Secondarily, they act as America's militia but over the years have seen multiple deployments in Afghanistan and Iraq. Whether you are a weekend soldier or one designated with a career commitment to military service, you are servants to the will of the government in how best they can use your service at home and abroad.

Chapter 3

It would not take long after arriving in Vietnam to have the paradigm shifted from any reluctance I may have had to embrace the unfamiliarity of an environment that posed a threat to my survival. As the plane was landing delivering another load of unsuspected souls on the beaten path of Cam Ranh Bay's runways so many had taken before me; the urgent request to disembark and run for cover caused me to shutter in fear. My insecurities instantly catapulted to a place my conscience refused to lead me; mortars, bullets and the induction of overwhelming fear.

It would be the beginning of many questions I would ponder during my tenure in the jungle; *"Would I make it home safely or would I be another statistic feathered in the hat of those sitting in the comfort of their living rooms watching television of a war thousands of miles away?"* I realized war makes no exception to accommodate any fears one may have. Only the strong survive to live another day. But even then, there are no guarantees with any degree of certainty you will ever see home again.

When I first saw the Vietnamese, I marveled at their meekness and generosity. They were indisputably nice people, humble and full of smiles; living a life of simplicity. When our eyes would encounter, there was an eerie sense rather unsettling to me. Why were they smiling amidst such turmoil and carnage? Was it genuine? My skepticism of their intentions began to escalate with growing cynicism when the nightly raids increased on our compound. After it was revealed that some of them were double agents; *"Agents of surveillance during the day before transforming into black pajama Ninjas during the night"*; I approached them with caution measuring my steps in every encounter.

Was it by choice they played such a role or were they constrained by fear of losing their villages, families or were they just profiteers capitalizing on American blood? I did not know them and knew nothing of their culture, but they knew me. I was the *"dark rider on a white horse"* bringing hope for the repression of the innocent.

The Vietnamese were just impassioned as I was in their struggle for freedom in pursuit of a life all their own. They wanted peace; peace from the aggression from the North; peace from our occupation using their country and struggles as a proxy for our own interest. Whether we have accepted this as truth, we also delivered terror into their lives by the misfortune of our arrogance and weapons of intimidation.

The cynical attitude I had of the Vietnamese was fueled primarily because of my resentment in being in a place I desired not to be. It would be much later I would discover that they knew more about my struggles as a *"Black Man"* than I knew of their repressive history. I did not fully understand their precarious predicament but this would be an encounter that would change my life more than theirs.

Based on my observation, I initially referred to the Vietnamese as *"The Little People"*. It was with no disrespect but a generalization relative to my perception of something I found quite intriguing. That's how stigmas begin when the reflections of our characterization in comparison to ourselves is exploited to the level of commonality. Our justification derives from the fact; *"If it doesn't look like me, act like me, think like me, it must be lesser than me"*. It's a flawed concept to believe that we can determine the value of another's existence relative to our perceptions and biases.

We all share in the indictment of having an exaggerated judgment of ourselves to believe we are something greater than we really are; *"Thinking of ourselves more highly than we ought to!"* Prolong exposure to that type of attitude will leave you with a *"superiority complex"* and if you allow it to fester, it will grow in intensity rising to the level of hatred, bigotry and prejudicial intolerance. The developmental process of intolerance usually begins early in childhood reflective of one's surroundings and indoctrinations before their conscience has had an opportunity to gain its own independent ideas and opinions free from the biases of others.

For some who were brought up in isolated environments, surrounded and reinforced by attitudes of indifference, negative infusions served only to compound years of frustrations to an already unconstructive way of thinking. Some succumb to bigotry and bias stemming from their ancestral roots while others resist the inclusion of principles so very different than their own. The wall of isolation produces ignorance. The result of ignorance is anchored in fear further separating from any hope of adaptability to accept changes in our ever evolving society.

Merriam-Webster's medical definition of a superiority complex defines it as being *"an excessive striving for or pretense of superiority to compensate for supposed inferiority."* Simply meaning the problem is not someone else's but a negative judgment of one's own beliefs, character and persona. The condescending attitude of those who adopt such an attitude will face an inevitable walk of reckoning. It will be as believing one can walk a ship's plank over the water blindfolded without falling. Odds are you will fall regardless of how high your head extends into the clouds.

Because of youthful folly and lack of knowing, I adopted the word *"Gook"* into my vocabulary as all of us did while not knowing its implications in reference to the Vietnamese. Gook is no different than the derogatory stigma of someone calling me the *"N"* word! Ignorance should not be an excuse since we all bleed the same, share in breathing the same atmosphere and have the same needs of security, prosperity and peace. We must always consider the value of our words and how we choose to use them. Our words have meaning directly linked to opinions and issues legislated on the tablets of our hearts that at times can be biasing to another.

 As I looked at the faces of the Vietnamese people, I could not have told you the difference from one or the other; from one mosquito to the next mosquito. I never got to know any of them by name; just *"Papa San and Momma San"*. On every occasion they referred to me as *"Number One Soul Brother"*. They had convinced me that was my name even though they considered me as being *"boo-coo dinky dau"* which literally means *"I wasn't just crazy but had completely lost my mind"*.

What separated North Vietnam from South Vietnam was an ideological geographical grid located on the 17th Parallel which determined who our enemy was. It is easy to separate the lines of demarcation when you see the directions of tracers flying at you in the heat of the night or mortars bombarding your base in the bright of day but in the silhouette of darkness, the images of an enemy are all the same.

As a Combat Veteran, some of my memories of Vietnam are embedded with emotions settled in great despair. War is ugly and it will reshape your psychophysical makeup that is very difficult to reverse. It is not always a given due to repetitive traumatic occurrences that you will ever be the same.

The emotional impact is not debatable; it is definitely life changing. Supplanting any contrary deduction is a tortuous attempt of denial. The slate of my mind will forever be stained with the blood of our Brothers which drained into the Earth in a foreign land beyond the hope of reclaiming. That sounds like the recipe for guilt which so many of us have endured throughout the years.

For some of us, if we knew the challenges we would face returning to the *"Free World"*, we could have easily considered refuge in another land. Broken lives, broken spirits wounded in every sense of the imagination. We were victims of servitude; a servant to our memories and wandering souls going to and fro searching to turn our nights into a brighter tomorrow. It has taken years of struggling to move beyond the liability of my disappointments to realize;

> *"I would rather see the sun in its rising than to be absent of light without the breath of redemption."*

It is better to have fallen and still have the opportunity to get up than to have fallen with no strength left to redeem.

Truth is truth and does not accept the variance of facts. Facts can be as variable in complexity as the changing leaves of the autumn trees. Truth stands as a pillar of stone, monumental as a high rising mountain. Conversely, the temporary nature of facts is a variable concept that is relative to one's perception that can change from one day to the next.

Some of our memories of the affairs of war are varied or were lost as time has gone by but the vast amount of them has left us with permanent impressions of ourselves and the value we give to other human beings. Impressions of war will forever be seared in our conscience. Even though years have passed, the memories still exist seemingly with an attrition that continues to wear away the fabric of our existence.

From the Killing Fields to the Playing Fields

After I left Vietnam I had a quick 2 week sabbatical in the *"Free World"* before heading for Germany to finish out my time. I guess the powers that be thought maybe a place of transition was necessary before my introduction back into the streets of America. I left Vietnam with my mind and emotions in a very volatile state. It was extremely difficult to harness the energy to continue on as a soldier yielding to an authority that never respected me. My conscience was seared with anger and venomous retaliation because of the way I was treated by *"Officers"* who cared little to none about me. I cannot truthfully say that the fault was all theirs; I wanted just be left alone and I felt justified (Chapter 4 pg. 50-52).

Germany is a very beautiful country. If it wasn't for the circumstances of my departure I honestly believe that I would have stayed. In contrast, it was worlds apart from the culture in Southeast Asia. I was never afforded the opportunity to see Vietnam through the eyes of neutrality; always one confrontation after another. For sure I did not miss leaving there; time didn't come soon enough.

After a few mishaps along the way, I finally arrived at a quaint little town in Germany called Ansbach. After getting checked in; the first thing I discovered; *"dress right dress didn't work for me"*. I thought they were nuts! I had just arrived from the battlefield; real bullets; real people dying; real fear. No mock exercises and no fake alerts. The audacity to play war was an insult! I never did find the motivation to fake it.

I had an afro larger than Angela Davis's revolutionary *"natural"*. I didn't shave in Vietnam but of course didn't grow too much hair on my face. I never shined my boots or brasso belt buckles; didn't starch my fatigues neither felt the need to blouse them. The jungle was not the environment to concern yourself with how well you were dressed. I could have died naked and they still would not have cared. Why should it have mattered if I still wore my black cross around my neck or my black wrist band instead of a watch? The days of teaching me how to be a soldier had run its course when I left the States for the battlefield.

I found myself lonelier in Germany than I had been at any time in Vietnam. Basically, I lived in the privacy of my own mind. There was no one who thought like me or shared in the same life experiences as I did. I was surrounded by people who enlisted to get out of going to Vietnam and they did; couldn't find anyone who had seen the battlefield. To my surprise I discovered that they were the privileged ones with the rite of passage to *"play Army"*. They were totally disconnected from what was going on oceans apart in Vietnam. It was as if there were two separate armies; plastic people on vacation while the other continued to bleed.

I was a misfit; living in a *"fool's paradise"*! Not because I desired to be but logistically, I was put into a system where I never should have been. It was purposed for my failure; to break me and remold me into an image of something I could never be. I had PTSD (toxic stress); suffering from battle fatigue with symptoms that traveled the oceans. I couldn't jump out of my skin and be something I wasn't! Couldn't sleep worth a damn and my nerves were fried crispier than a potato. I was sick and they laughed! It would not have mattered where I was; the results would have been the same. Little did I know the resentment I felt could not compare to what was waiting for me back home.

I left Germany as a broken man; broken in every way imaginable. After receiving an *"Undesirable Discharge"* my world spiraled into depths I had never known. Handcuffed to a military escort, I traveled back across the ocean to an unwelcomed America still grieving from its own grief. After processing out at Ft. Dix N.J., I was escorted to the front gate and again was told of my suspended rights; as a veteran, as a citizen, as a human being.

The *"silent wounds"* of combat are real. It does not take a rocket scientist to decipher a psychological profile of the wounded. Pain is pain; grief is grief; blood bleeds red and fear is a terror that can exceed its boundaries leading to torment. There are no measuring tools available to accurately determine the toll that war can have on any human being. Baselines established prior to war for any soldier entering the battlefield and exiting with an examination of debriefings, cannot account for the toll it takes on one's families, friends and familiar circles of acquaintances.

It would be years later President Jimmy Carter exonerated those who chose to flee America because of their refusal to participate in a conflict that had nothing to do with the security of America's democracy. We stigmatized them as being *"Draft Dodgers"*! They were no different than some of our Politicians who are currently holding the spotlight amplifying their cowardliness with rhetorical absurdity.

As a consequence of Carter's decision, my discharge was upgraded to *"Honorable"* to reflect my service of wartime engagement which we now call the *"Vietnam Era"*. I was reinstated with benefits that up until then had been denied to thousands of Vietnam Veterans who were in theater. I have often contemplated the reasons why the United States Government adopted such a policy as to deny recognition of honorable service to the multitudes who served in a conflict that cost so much American blood. What a betrayal! We were boys made into men by prescription of policies that produced irrevocable damage to the lives of so many of our veterans. For some, their scattered remains were laid to waste in a land without conscience of their sacrifice.

As many as 80,000 veterans who suffered from post-traumatic stress and received other than honorable discharges can use evidence of their PTSD to petition service boards to upgrade the bad paper discharge. At stake for individuals is removal of lifelong stigmas that have scarred reputations, limited job prospects and blocked critical veteran benefits. Defense Secretary Chuck Hagel this month directed that boards for correction of military records or naval records begin to "fully and carefully consider every petition based on PTSD brought by each veteran." His Sept. 3 memo gives Army, Navy and Air Force secretaries "supplemental guidance" that boards are to use when petitioners seek discharge upgrades claiming that unrecognized Post-Traumatic Stress Disorder caused the misbehavior that led to Other Than Honorable discharge. Many of the veterans who will gain from the new guidance served during the **Vietnam War, before the medical community recognized PTSD as a disabling service-connected condition.** *PTSD received a medical diagnostic code only in 1980, five years after that war officially ended. Hagel instructed boards to give "liberal consideration" to any language found in medical records describing one or more symptoms that meet diagnostic criteria for PTSD or related conditions. Liberal consideration also is to be used when veterans' civilian providers have diagnosed PTSD. And where PTSD "is reasonably determined to have existed at the time of discharge," it is to be "a mitigating factor" in the misconduct that generated an other than honorable, also then called undesirable discharge.*
http://www.nj.com/mercer/index.ssf/2014/09/military_update_80000_vets_with_ptsd_could_gain_discharge_upgrades.html

Returning Home

Upon my return home I thought I would be left alone. The FBI had other plans for reasons I choose not to qualify in this writing. I never did anything but what my country asked me to do! Why was I being punished with so much disrespect and vitriol? When I left Vietnam, I loaded my baggage onto the *"Flying Tiger"*, all of my baggage; physical, mental and emotional baggage which took ten years to unpack. The thought to search amongst the ruins to recover whatever I could never occurred to me because of fear of what would be uncovered. At times truth is very difficult to embrace when we may have fallen and begin to measure the cost of courage to face the extraordinary events surrounding our lives.

I had become psychosomatic; trapped within myself, hurting, screaming for help; anybody's help to relieve me of the misery I found myself living. I pleaded for mercy but my voice fell upon deafened ears. Empathetic gestures of support came from family and friends but no one knew how deep my problems were. So much of me was left on the shores of an unforgiving continent but still close enough to the haunting memories I tried so desperately to forget.

In my ponderings with reflections seemingly so close as yesterday, I still feel undeserving anguish from rejection that had catapulted me into pursuing a life void significantly of meaning; *"Ten years of 'significance lost searching for a meaning of my existence to place my name amongst the living".*

War is painful; not always forgiving. I believe it is the most humbling undertaking anyone could ever engage in. The consequences can be entangling, clutching as an octopus tentacles as we've often struggled to get free from that place called yesterday. Thomas Hobbes a notable psychologist wrote that war is also an attitude:

*"By war is meant a state of affairs, which may exist even while its operations are **not continued**;"*
(I.E. Encyclopedia of Philosophy; "IEP.ut.edu/war")

"Exist even while its operations are not continued"! This is the attitude of so many veterans I have come to know including myself of the battles confronting us every day; the battle of the war of our memories; the hurt and pain, physical afflictions and the emotional suffering from the experience of trauma on a battlefield that still exist in continuum. The daily triggers of intrusive thoughts are ever so prevalent and will not allow the luxury of normalcy regardless of how deep we may search.

War changes things and it changes people. It changes those whom we've come to serve and it changes our own lives sometimes for better or worse. No two lives are the same. There is no cookie cutter of predictability in our response to any given set of circumstances. As a result of our participation, believe it or not some of us remained enslaved to the enticing thirst for blood; that is to say they would do it again in reversal of their involvement and still not accept any remorse for destroying another's life. There are others who are living pretentious lives of denial who will curse the idea of accepting any claim of responsibility for having ever been in Vietnam. In either situation, the glass ceiling of reality needs to be shattered into an awakening to accept the presentation of life on its own terms.

For the vast majority of us, the choices we make when confronting life's challenges can be somewhat limiting due to the battle scars and unhealed wounds that have cut so deeply unraveling the fragile threads that are holding our emotions together. The oozing of anxiety will eventually overflow resulting in a spontaneous outburst of anger; temporarily suppressing our cognitive thoughts and sound judgment. When we lash out at the world as we fume with anger, at some point humility will descend upon us and we will be faced with the choice to accept the solution that will begin the process of healing. *"Forgive ourselves and forgive those who have perpetrated our downfall"*. It may be the most humbling thing we could have ever considered; but I am convinced, there is deliverance in Truth.

In seeking solutions I have done as many of you, resorting to past behaviors that were familiar and convenient; drugs, alcohol and drugs of the self medicating kind. The choices we made led to consequences that altered our psychophysical makeup with the closing stages resulting in anxiety and depressive disorders. Anxiety will always have a mind of its own and certainly depression will keep you occupied in a stupor surrounded by every bad choice imaginable. It is a very dangerous place to be; separated and isolated with only misery as your company reflecting as a mirror of a defeated future not worth the effort to engage.

For that reason, as reported on CNN's Nightly News, Combat Veterans are committing suicide at an alarming rate. Without answers to vacate the imprisonment of their misery, nearly 22 veterans are taking their lives daily as the only solution to be found. This is a sad testament of a country who vowed to take care of their veterans regardless of the price to rehabilitate our Wounded Warriors and bring restitution into their lives and families. The routine occurrences of the affairs of life afforded those who have never experienced the anguish of the battlefield can't compare to the bittersweet confrontations Combat Veterans face on a daily basis.

Move On

There are long standing circumstances confronting us daily that must be eradicated before we can move forward without the liability of our past continuing to haunt us. The consequences of war have predisposed us to susceptibility of failure; failure in our families, relationships, finances, careers as well as an impediment to our motivations and dreams.

Some of our mountainous trepidations existed before we were even conceived which only served to compound any recover attempt we pursued. Regrettably, we inherit those things as our legacy. As a consequence, we tend to take ownership of things not pertaining significantly to our affairs. Dysfunction is prevalent in all of our lives which we can easily impose upon others, mainly those who are close to us. Every battle is not ours to fight. There are some things pertaining to life we are rendered powerless in our attempts to control.

Every day of living offers its own set of challenges and does not need the burdening of any vulnerabilities attaching to our already fragile emotional state. How undeserving! However, what's considered undeserving to one can prove to be a catalyst to another. As human beings, it all matters as to how our perspectives have been shaped and the conclusions we've made along life's journey. When the persuasions of outside influences no longer affects the swaying of our conscience of its ability to maintain balance, our predisposed susceptibilities will minimize to be of little significance.

As veterans, we've endured more than our share of suffering, dysfunction and even grief that somehow were so overwhelming that it turned into something greater in the later years of our lives. These reminders are ever before us and we face them daily as a consequence of our participation in a war that seemingly has no end. When we build upon a foundation mired in negativity, our circumstances will develop significantly in intensity with our state of affairs spiraling out of control proving to be of greater consequence.

Chapter 4

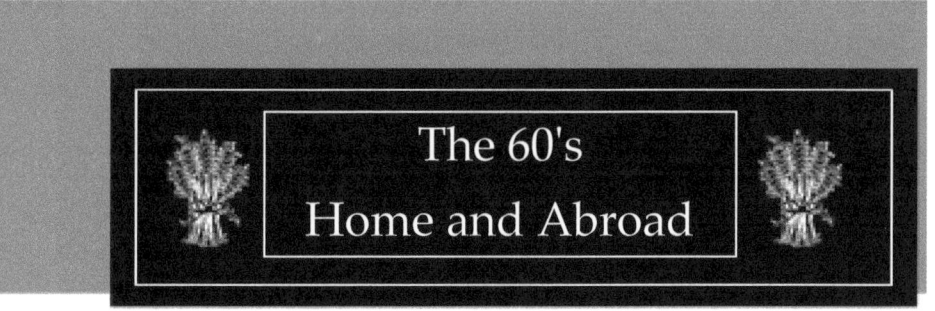

The 60's
Home and Abroad

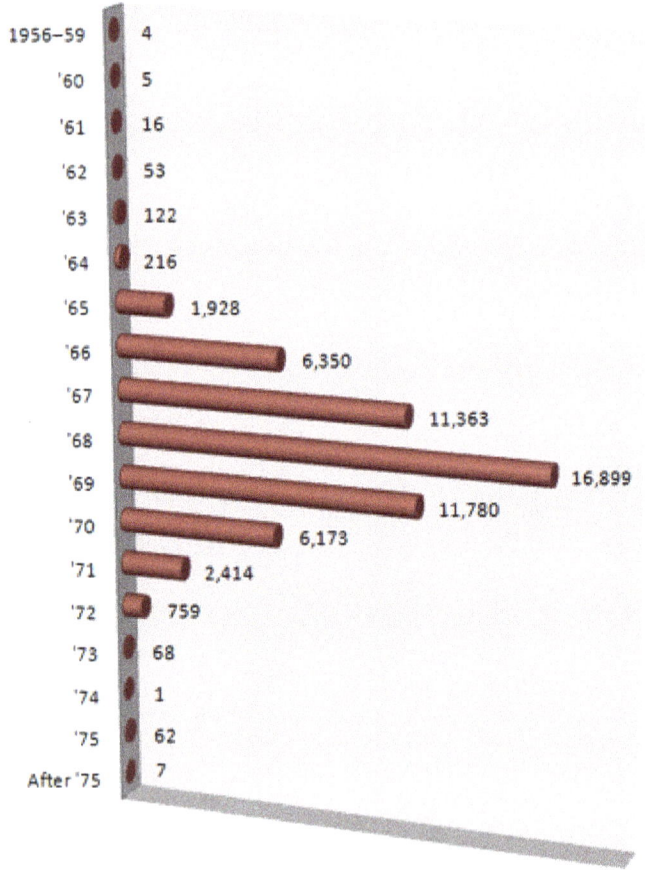

DCAS Vietnam Conflict Extract File record counts by INCIDENT OR DEATH DATE (Year)

www.archives.gov/research/military/vietnam-war/casualty-statistics.html

The power of separatism negates the principle of equality when rendered on the scales of justice. It establishes boundaries of inequality; the premise of a lesser and a greater; a wiser or a smarter; one seceding from the other. Simply putting it; it is a recipe for chaos and confusion waiting to happen on any battlefield.

The social climate of America back in the 60's was chaotic to say the least. The Civil Rights movement was at its peak at the same time organizations such as NAACP, SCLC, the Black Panthers, the Nation of Islam and the Black Nationalist Movement had colliding interest in pursuit of answers for Black equality.

The KKK and the White Citizens Council of the 60's had their heyday as well as home grown terrorist with their campaign of bombing schools, churches and any place defined as a house of freedom. Lynching and burnings on sacrificial crosses can only compare to the mayhem we see happening today across the Middle East of the horrifying images of beheadings and assassinations. It is astonishing realizing that these events happened just 50 years in our not so distant past right here in *"The United States of America"*. Nowadays, we have electronic social media which instantly exposes the horrors and fears being exacerbated around the globe of the brutality of war and oppression by governmental societies.

Today, there is a cry for *"Black Lives Matter"* and rightfully so as it also should be the cry for the life of every American that matters. However, *"Institutional Racism"* has no parallel. If we have learnt anything from the lessons of our history, despite the appearance of turmoil brewing in the dark houses of revolt, we are still *"One Nation, under God, Indivisible with Liberty and Justice for All and not only for the Biased Privileged"*.

The brutal acts of terrorism being committed today around the globe against men, women and even children are synonymous with the vitriol of the 60's against Blacks here in America. Innocent Black children slaughtered in the houses of learning and in church pews of neutrality eventually met the appeal from around the world.

Assassinations of Black leaders were instigated to stem the tide of a revolution spiraling out of control. Dr. Martin Luther King lost his life, amongst other reasons, in opposition to the massacres of our sons in a senseless war displayed on the nightly news of all of our major networks.

King had been a solid supporter of President <u>Lyndon B. Johnson</u> and his Great Society, but he became increasingly concerned about U.S. involvement in Vietnam and, as his concerns became more public, his relationship with the Johnson administration deteriorated. King came to view U.S. intervention in Southeast Asia as little more than imperialism. Additionally, he believed that the <u>Vietnam War</u> diverted money and attention from domestic programs created to aid the black poor. Furthermore, he said, 'the war was doing far more than devastating the hopes of the poor at home... **We were taking the black young men who had been crippled by our society and sending them eight thousand miles away to guarantee liberties in Southeast Asia which they had not found in southwest <u>Georgia</u> and East Harlem..........'"** *King maintained his antiwar stance and supported peace movements until he was assassinated on April 4, 1968, one year to the day after delivering his Beyond Vietnam speech.*
http://www.history.com/this-day-in-history/

Day after day, our American soldiers continued to lose their lives seemingly in a war that would never end. In the 1968 Tet Offensive, 245 of our brethren lost their lives in one day and virtually 2500 in one month's time. Having opposed *"the powers that be"*, Dr. King's voice threatened the coffers of the profiteers whose only interest was financial gain stained with American blood. Consequently, his life came to an end by a conspiracy revoking the continuation of life's privilege of the <u>Right to Be</u>. *"When was and is free speech truly free?"* It's free when those of entitlement give sanctions of acceptance as not to incur a burden of cost.

> *The Vietnam War was a "huge cash cow" for the establishment elite in the areas of oil, the military-industrial complex and the banks.*
> http://www.bibliotecapleyades.net/sociopolitica/

At no time in our history had we seen the dynamic of a domestic conflict fought with weapons so diametrically opposed. This movement would be different; *"Non Violent"* even though I beg to differ with the discriminating analysis of whose blood was being sacrificed.

The police departments across this land who were sworn to protect us were complicit in their direct participation by ignoring the laws of liberty they made an oath to enforce. From the days of Richard Nixon's police state to eliminate subversive organizations such as the Black Panthers with fear and intimidation, as of today, that culture still exist.

On America's killing fields that have claimed so much blood of its own since its inaugural beginnings, a war was fought not with guns and bullets but by intellectual engagement at the highest level of our society. *"Ideas don't have boundaries if they are respected for what they truly are."* Ultimately, the ideas that were framed instigated peace giving all citizens voting rights and access to houses of higher learning. By empowering those who previously were left out of the process has served our country well. However, a recent ruling by the Supreme Court weakened protections of the 1965 Voting Rights Act. The striving ambition of every American citizen is centered on the principles guaranteed in our constitution; *"Life, Liberty and the Pursuit of Happiness."*

The protocols embedded in our court system of equal access and justice is the last battle to be fought. Our framework of laws and their constitutional interpretation are being measured by an elite few. If you are affluent in this country (Affluenza), there is the likelihood a different standard of law will apply. If you are the underrepresented of our society such as veterans, the poor or one of a minority persuasion, the deck is stacked decidedly against you.

Shatter the Silence

In Vietnam, there was a parallel that mimicked the streets of America in the 60's. From base camp to base camp you would see the separation. Black Brothers (*The Bloods*) hung with Black Brothers as well as White Brothers hanging with their own. Brothers wearing black wrist bands, black crosses, afros and giving up *"dap"* to one another were the calling cards indicative of those who were involved in the struggle. The term *"Dapping"* was admission into the brotherhood; an agreement of unity and defiance. With our hands slapping, fingers snapping, foot stomping, chest thumping and fist pumping measured as chatter in the winds of a revolution. Those ceremonial greetings were undeniably intimidating echoing a voice of discontent to the *"Powers of Injustice"*.

Away from base camp back into the killing fields, *"psychoses of togetherness"* returned. Everybody was one again all fighting for the survival of each other. It proved a valuable lesson: *"In time of war our sacrifices are the same; we bleed the same; we hurt with the same agonizing tears of disillusioning when our emotions are shattered in disbelief"*. However, when it's time to exercise our individual choices, regrettably we tend to retreat to our own patriotic corner of ethnicity.

During the social revolution of the 60's, we saw the landscape change from segregation to government enforced tolerance of desegregation. Segregation literally refers to *"legal and social"* enforcement separating African Americans from their Caucasian (White) counterparts. Discriminatory racial practices against people of color were implemented by Jim Crow laws which were passed after the Reconstruction Era. They invoked sweeping reforms denying voting rights, education, housing, fairness in the market place and expunged any advancements achieved within the Black community. I have lived long enough to have drunk out of *"colored only water fountains, pissed in colored only toilets, learning in colored only schools."* Remember the Tuskegee Airmen? They were symbolic of America's hypocrisy.

Technically, after segregation had ended, the general populous of White America, particularly in the southern states and our urban cities, instigated a revolution of their own; *"White Flight"*. In principal, they embraced the doctrine of *"Isolationism"* where Whites who rejected the government's enforced inclusion of Blacks into the mainstream of our society fled America's cities creating their own communities in suburbs (sub-urban). With them went their wealth abandoning the concept of inclusion which was necessary to sustain a peaceful alliance of government and all its citizens. Appropriations for funding and distribution never reached the balance sheets of equality. The result of *"White Flight"* further divided an already volatile relationship.

The infrastructure of our major cities began to crumble. The central districts surrounding the economic centers of our cities where the majority of Blacks lived suffered from one budgetary crisis after another. The ones that were harmed the most were our children who were left with second tier educational resources and suffocating dreams with no other choice of fulfilling their aspirations in life. Crime, drugs, unemployment and broken families were significant byproducts of a system resolved to failure and the battle still continues.

The doctrine of separatism only served those within the White community to pacify and deny life's privileges to the minority interest in this country. Yet again, we see this struggle being played out right before our eyes. Don't believe me? *"Ask any Latino."* The attitudes of indifference towards them by a segment of our society who are bound to the principles of exclusion are repeats from yesterday's playbook.

From Bible to Verse

I entered Vietnam with a Bible tucked under my arm. It wasn't soon after that I became disenchanted with my faith. Somehow the idea of killing for a cause I could not justify distorted my belief. Needless to say, I had a battle back home to fight. The Vietnamese had never done anything to me. At every turn they called me *"Number One Soul Brother"*. What did they do to rise to the level of an offense? Somehow, they saw a distinction that we both shared of common credence. They were struggling as I was and knew my history of suffrage in the land of the free; *"America"*. What was done in the dark became visible for the world to see that we both were viewed as second class citizens.

Lies and disparaging opinions concerning my humanity were broadcasted abroad as a propaganda tool of humiliation. It proved to be a catalyst of defiance propelling me into a sphere of intolerance. I soon became a radical sympathizer supporting the struggle for Black respect and equality.

Laying my Bible aside, I adopted a new text that appealed to the delicate balance of my conscience; *"Soul on Ice"*. The author Eldridge Clever believed in armed insurrection and flirted with the idea of a Black separatist state as the only way to achieve racial equality. At first glance, his ideas appeared to be rather extreme; however I accepted a truth I wanted so desperately to change. He exploited the idea that had classified lower class Black men with strong bodies as being a *"Super Masculine Menial"*. The implications were quite strong as a reminder of the days of my ancestors who came to this country as slaves classified as two-thirds human void of the methodical skills of reasoning. Putting it simply; *"A Body but No Brains"*.

To be labeled intellectually disadvantaged was an insult I combated with vehement resistance. Like the *"Scare Crow"* of the Wizard of Oz who never had a brain and was determined to find his way down the *"Yellow Brick Road"*; I was persistent in my actions of being recognized for being more than a strong body of iron. I demanded the respect of being no different than any other human being; no lesser or greater but the *"Right to Be"*! The paradigm had shifted. I became a freedom fighter but not for the cause I was sent to do.

There are times as we sift through the murkiness and confusion of war, our perspectives will be challenged and we can become cynical and disillusioned when we get exposed to carnage instigated by weapons designed for maximum infliction, sometimes on the innocent. War will drive you deeper in search for justification; searching for comfort relative to your own understanding. Just as the *Scare Crow* without a brain to think for himself, we were as pawns in a game of chess without a voice to be heard.

Agreement in any war is a principle of survival. On the dark side, some of our soldiers lost their lives due to *"fragging"*. Fragging occurs when one soldier turns on another with intent to murder or maim. Unrealistic as one could imagine, that was the culture in Vietnam. Incidents of fragging were quite common usually targeting officers who had been to *"West Point"* who came with their own agendas. The practicality of war is not effectuated in a classroom of theory but on the battlefield where blood sacrifices are offered up daily. Improvisations never scripted on the tables of any war room at times take precedent over conventional approaches. The jungle can teach you many things as well as the *"Urban Warfare"* of the Middle East.

There were two indiscriminate attempts to inflict serious physical harm on my life and not by our prescribed enemy. One was the decision of a Commanding Officer who subjected me to a suicidal assignment. Initially I complied not knowing the danger of the conditions. After hearing explosions going off around me, I abandoned the assignment for fear of my life. Consequently, I was Court-martialed with a charge of *"Insubordination and Assault on a "Superior Officer"*.

Little did I know what was waiting for me. I was put in solitary confinement in a Conex shipping container until the time of my trial. For you who do not know what that is; it is a tractor trailer container made into a makeshift jail reinforced with iron bars. Who dreamed up that crazy stuff; confined in 100 degree sweltering heat and daily incoming rocket attacks? When the rockets came all the guards ran for cover and left me defenseless like a caged animal. No weapons to defend myself; nowhere to run. I was a sitting duck trapped inside a container of iron bars. How inhumane! Was I scared? *"Hell Yeah! I was Traumatized!"*

I survived nearly 2 months incarceration; not on my own but with the help of *"The Brothers"* who would sneak vials of contraband through the holes in the slabs of iron. I stayed high from one day to the next; snorting my brains out like a race horse snorting for air. That was my only hope of maintaining my sanity throughout that ordeal. By the way truth be told; I beat the charges and was warned of the consequences waiting for me. Retaliation came immediately and with a vengeance I did not expect. I was stripped of my ranking without cause and shuffled on a C-130 going south.

It wasn't too long after arriving at my new location that the feeling of despondency began to set in. I was losing it. My emotions were in a tizzy. I wanted to go home so desperately. I was tired; tired of fighting; tired of people; tired of the same old routine. By then, I was a short timer biding my time to get back to the *"Free World"*.

It would not take long to discover that prejudice and racism has no boundaries. Geographically, from north to south; east to west, biases are not contained by borders; not even the cerebral borders of a sick mind. If you recall, after the 9/11 attack on our country, all of America came together and stood as *"one"*. One mind; one body united in the same spirit. How long did that last? In times of conflict, we do come together for the common good of each other, but when the smoke settles, the contrary winds encompassing our discontent further divides us deeper into our ethnic strongholds. It is a continual battle seemingly without end.

The second attempt made upon my life came by the hands of one of our own; a fellow soldier; a Caucasian Brother. He stood outside my hut and emptied a full magazine from his M16 Assault Rifle through the walls where I was sitting. The use of deadly force was an attempt to murder me without regard for my life and the only enemy was my music. Regrettably, my response was swift with a rage I desire never to see again. I never did learn of his predicament but what I do know is the next day I was on a plane heading back to the States. Still as of today, I cannot fathom a reason for his provocation; I was in my own space exercising my *"Right to Be"*. Perhaps it was the message of my music; *"Buffalo Soldier living in the streets called America"*. Who hates Bob Marley? At times, the rhythm of our music carries a louder message than any words we could ever say.

In Vietnam because of the separation between Whites and Blacks, you were stigmatized by the style of music you played. In truth, music kept us connected to the *"Free World"* by offering temporary moments of escape. Being from the South, I grew up listening to *"Soul, Gospel and Rock 'n' Roll"* music but somehow I never acquired a fondness for Hillbilly Music; it didn't appeal to me. Tobacco spitting rebel yellers were never akin to my interest. That was not my culture. I am from the South but not that South.

I never did have an appreciation for the rousers who couldn't handle their alcohol turning them into pretenders with an appearance of strength. Simply putting it; they were *"perpetrating a fraud"* using alcoholic spirits as a provocation to act out of character. Furthermore, who would have wanted to drink liquor in the mosquito infested heat of Vietnam? Heat and alcohol don't mix; together they will vaporize your brain and disarm you of your senses. Vietnam provided the opportunity of drinking all the alcohol you could handle and smoke as much weed as you wanted. It was a very simple choice for me; *"I spent my whole tour fumigated with the herbs of the Earth. After all, they were all natural even the opium".*

A Cultural Shift

America in the 60's was undergoing a cultural and moral revolution. It was reflected in the ethnicity and music of the Haight-Ashbury Hippie generation. Free love and free sex emerged out of the subculture as the new norm. It was a time of liberation, a step away from the traditions of yesterday. During those rebellious times of experimentation, your drug of choice identified the type of music you listened to. From the acid rock of Jimmy Hendrix's *"Purple Haze"* to the soul sensations of the Temptation's *"My Girl"*, everyone danced to the new sounds of the times.

Our most recent wars brought its own set of issues to the battlefield. The issue of women participation and the most heated confrontation; *"Don't Ask Don't Tell"*. It has been said; *"A thought is never separated from its thinker."* Might I suggest to you, the babblings of our tongue does not always give indication of truth at the core of our being. What was being asked of the soldiers of different sexual orientation was *"denial by silence; don't say a babbling word"*. That seemed very troubling to say the least. Vietnam Veterans never had the homosexual issue to deal with. Men were just men; men of tradition doing what men always do. At the time, it was not an American subject that had surfaced onto the playing fields. To have been a homosexual would have gotten you a deferment in the draft.

For the most part I never saw a woman of American origin in Vietnam except for Bob Hope's USO Review and the nurses that treated me for multiple dehydrations from all the drugs I was taking. As for women; drugs and fear pacified my natural instinct, curbing any desire of attraction to the opposite sex. After 7 months in the combat theater, I took an R&R *(Rest and Relaxation)* to Hong Kong. It was then I regained my humanity and the joy bells were ringing again. They rang so loud that I went AWOL *(Absent Without Leave)*. I really didn't want to see Vietnam ever again. But my better senses prevailed and I reluctantly returned.

Vietnamese women didn't receive the respect from American soldiers. Rapes occurred quite frequently and prostitution was the same as in any previous wars. The idea of women wearing black silk pajamas bottoms and coned straw hats never appealed to me. They were in sharp contrast to the women wearing miniskirts promenading the streets of Seattle at the time when I left for Vietnam. Traditionally, the Vietnamese women worked in the fields growing rice as their main staple. They bore the misfortune of adapting American ways supplanting their traditional culture in hope of landing on the shores of America's promise land. Somehow, I really don't blame them. After 7 million tons of bombs dispersed on your land; who wouldn't want to leave. Restitution has always been a major part of our foreign policy but not always reconciliation. Since when have we gone into a war and gave a damn about forgiveness. We insist on imposing our rule! We've always justified our wrongs even to the detriment of those we say we've come to help.

Changing of Attitudes

Today in our Vet Centers, brothers are not identified by the color of their skin, but the common bond of suffering we've all endured. We have come to realize without unity as we struggle for fairness, separatism will only hinder our advancement with a greater divergence. Collectively, we embrace the years of our sufferings all in search for the fleeting moments of laughter we so desperately need.

Veterans are human beings as anyone else. However, there is a drastic difference in the life of a soldier compared to the majority of our populous who have never been directly exposed to the threats and insecurities of war. Though our life experiences may differ, we share the same values as any *"American"* with the difference being we made a decision to bear the torch of freedom in defense of our democracy; to go where not everyone desires to go.

Dr. Martin Luther King Jr.

"America is essentially a dream. It is a dream of a land of Men of all Races, all Nationalities and all Creeds can live together as Brothers. The Brotherhood of Man will become a reality; Transforming dark destiny into a bright tomorrow. In 'This Day' We will be able to achieve 'This New Day'."

At times his words get lost in the arrogance of a reality which refuses to change. Despite the division that continues to grip this country; *"I choose to dream"*. What good is peace without the freedom to live a life of dignity and pride? Why must a man continually be judged by the color of his skin rather than the character that is in his heart? Why must a life be sacrificed at the expense of one's ideas that can move the heart and soul of a nation away from bigotry and prejudice?

From the mountain top of hope in search of justice to an assignment of death leading a garbage worker's strike for fairness in the market place; the atmosphere is still charged with inhaling particles of life ready for a new revolution;

"I Still Have a Dream"

"A revolution of love and ideas annihilating the contempt of war; not fear but peace as attainable as your next inhaling breath. It's a choice; we can choose life and live in peace or remain divided with an ambiguous conscience unequally balanced on the scales of justice.

Chapter 5

The youngest to die in Vietnam; Dan Bullock, US Marine Corps who was 15 years old. (3)

I have a medical condition I have been battling that the Veterans Administration had diagnosed as hereditary. I knew then it was unlikely because no one in my family's history had ever suffered from that issue; not saying it is not possible. But I understood the VA's track record in how they do business. I knew in my heart it was an attempt on their part to shrug from their responsibility; not bearing any ownership for concerns of liability issues. Remember, I said *"It's all about Money; Fat Cats who continue to get fat without having put any skin in the game"*. They haven't changed and never will until the mindset of our populous shift from the mundane acceptance of our service to view us with equality just as any other veteran who served our country.

It was rather humorous after asking other doctors about my condition and the reported diagnosis. They never heard of it! It was something they had to research. That reminds me, when I was discharged from the military, I was immediately diagnosed with a nervous disorder. *Nervous Disorder?* Then why in the hell didn't I get a medical discharge rather than being rendered undesirable? The only nervous disorder I had was the craziness of Vietnam; crazy people doing crazy things to other people. If it were to be told what one human being can do to another in the common interest of war, to some it may seem quite horrifying.

I don't subscribe to be an alarmist raising a red flag at every junction. However, I did not accept the opinion of the VA. Doctors are only practitioners who do no acclaim to have mastered every diagnostic condition of the human anatomy. In my heart I had always believed it was the result of toxic chemicals, Agent Orange (AO) which had compromised my health in more ways than any diagnoses of predictability. The quality of service afforded to every Veteran should be more than being a number or who's next in line but service with dignity and respect as a valued human being.

It was finally determined that I had a growth on one of my glands that was causing the problem and not anything equating to heredity. Subsequently, I was denied a claim because of the weight of the VA doctor's diagnosis. Does that sound familiar? In light of this; what recourse do we have? It is easy to walk away brooding upon rejection after rejection but it is a much more difficult path to consider when you are dealing with a bureaucracy.

AO is a deadly killer. It does not reach the level of conspicuousness until you are so far downstream, then it's too late. Sometimes it takes years before the symptoms appear from the toxins that have invaded our bodies. With certainty, AO will always have a hold on our destiny.

> *Agent Orange is **one** of the herbicides and defoliants used by the U.S. military as part of its herbicidal warfare program, Operation Ranch Hand,[1] during the Vietnam War from 1961 to 1971 During the Vietnam War, between 1962 and 1971, the United States military sprayed nearly **20,000,000 U.S. gallons** (75,700,000 L) of chemical herbicides and defoliants in Vietnam, eastern Laos and parts of Cambodia, as part of the aerial defoliation program known as Operation Ranch Hand.[39][40] Like the British did in Malaya, the goal was to defoliate rural/forested land, depriving guerrillas of food and cover and clearing sensitive areas such as around base perimeters.[41] The program was also a part of a general policy of forced draft urbanization, which aimed to destroy the ability of peasants to support themselves in the countryside, forcing them to flee to the U.S. dominated cities, depriving the guerrillas of their rural support base.* http://en.wikipedia.org/wiki/Agent_Orange

Twenty million gallons of liquid death sprayed on the unsuspected. Little did I know at the time, those orange clouds falling from the sky on our food, water and clothing had such a toxic effect. I recall leaflets being dropped as a warning that the iron birds of prey would be coming to disperse tonnage of the casualty causing contaminant that would claim lives far into the future. As of today unsuspecting diseases are still claiming lives, mostly cancerous. AO has compromised not only our health, but the health of our children as a result of altering our DNA.

Diabetes has risen at an alarming rate for Vietnam Vets. The Veterans Administration has determined that diabetes is one of 14 diseases caused by herbicide exposure of AO with an endless list of secondary complications the VA considers presumptive. It wasn't presumptive at the time these agents were first employed but a known fact of science they were deadly killers. How deceptive! If you were in theater meaning you had boots on the ground, it is likelihood that at some point in your future, your health will be compromised.

President John F. Kennedy authorized the initiation of the U.S. Air Force herbicide program in Vietnam dating back to 1961 which continued until 1971. During my research, I discovered something I never knew; *"Agent Orange was not the only chemical herbicide used in Vietnam"*. A host of other toxins were used, some mimicking nerve agents and cancer causing carcinogens.

Our government is without excuse knowing the level of deliberation prior to the implementation of such a program. They knew in advance the consequences of environmental modification techniques that would inevitably compromise every soldier whose feet were planted in the jungle. Those who ate, drank and breathe the poisons had no clue they were endangering their lives. The Vietnamese still are suffering without any recourse of accountability from the US chemical companies that ravished their country.

It is my belief that the veterans who were in theater in what was considered hotspots are beneficiaries of 50 years of toxins lodged in their bodies. What an unwelcomed epithet that has claimed the lives of thousands and still counting.

Chemical	Active Ingredients	%age	Period of Use
Agent Pink	n-Butyl Ester 2,4,5,T	60%	1962-1964
	iso-Butyl Ester 2.4.5.-T	40%	
Agent Green	n-Butyl Ester 2.4.5.-T		1962-1964
Agent orange I & II	n-Buty Ester 2,4,-D	50%	1965-1970
	n-Butyl Ester 2,4,5,-T	50%	
Agent Purple	n-Butyl Ester 2,4,-D	50%	1962-1964
	n-Butyl Ester 2,4,5,-T	30%	
	iso-Butyl Ester 2,4,5,-T	200	
Agent White (Tordon 101)	Triisopropanolamine salt 2,4,-D		1965-1971
	Tri-isopropanlamine salt of Picloran		
Agent Blue (Phytar 5606)	Sodium Cacodylate	27.5%	1962-1970
	Free Cacodylic acid	4.8%	
Borate-Chlorate	Borate & Chlorate salts of alkaline metals		
Dalipon	2,2 Dichloroproponic acid		
Dinoxol	Butoxy Ethanol Ester 2.4.-D	200	
	Butoxy Ethanol Ester 2,4,5,-T	200	
Distillate Creosote	Diesoline	5%	1966-1967
	Creosote		(by Australia)
Diuron	3-9(3,4-Dichlorophenyl)-1 1-Dinethylurea		
Gramoxone (Paraquat)	Dinethyl Dipyridyl		1967 (by Australia)
Hyvar (Bromocil)	Butyl Methyluracil		
Monuron	Chlorphenyl Dimethlurea		
PicloraN			

http://vvanz.com/chemicals_list_vv_war.html

Veterans vs. VA

Vietnam Veterans have been besieged for years seeking rightful justice from determinations rendered by the Veterans Administration in their adjudication of congressional laws. Their ambiguous policies and controversial approach to delay and deny has raised so much havoc in the lives of too many veterans. VA's philosophy mirrors the image; *"You are determined guilty until your innocence is proven with the burden of proof transferred onto the veteran"*. Congress and the decision makers lack a clear, enforceable and consistent foundation of universal standards designed to expedite fairness towards us. For the most part, those who are in positions of authority writing and administering veteran's law have never seen a day of combat in their lives. They are distant from the true issues concerning us but are quick to render lip service; *"Thank You For Your Service"*.

> Eberhard Arnold wrote in his book titled "Inner Land":
> *"Only true weights give the conscience any value. Without them it keeps on vibrating and wavering unsteadily, deceiving and misleading in the most dangerous way. Only absolute truth gives the conscience any authority or guarantee of being right. The truth and what the truth demand in life is all that the conscience can represent with confidence.... The most carefully thought-out legislation is pernicious if it cannot prove itself before the conscience to be an objective expression of absolute justice."*

Judicial appointments are a key part of the process of controlling the least represented of our society. It's a buyer's market; *"Who do you know and how much influence you have."* Our Supreme Court has resorted to political activism embracing agendas of the elite. A Veteran's Service is the most valued investment of any country! At whatever the cost for reconciliation, judicial mitigation of veteran issues should take precedence over those who only engage in talking points of patriotism. We're not commodities and the laws of restitution should reflect the significance of our valued service. I still remain unconvinced of our *"Founders"* intention of *"One Law that applies to all equal in distribution"*.

Returning Vets from the Middle East

No disrespect to the veterans who have and are returning from the killing fields of the Middle East; as a Vietnam Vet I felt slighted in a certain way when I saw the respect of the American citizenry as well as veteran's organizations give in honor of their service.

One day while watching the news, I intently observed the greeting committees waiting at the airport for their return with flowers of love and gifts to bear with the red carpet rolled out welcoming back home America's heroes of a foreign war. The truth of it is buried in my pain. I wept! It had awakened the pain of distain we received returning home from Vietnam. It is my hope that never again should an American soldier has to suffer such a wicked betrayal.

You would have thought that America, the land of the free who proclaims its *"Exceptionalism"* would have never committed the unforgiveable sin of abandoning her own. The shouts of baby killers, morons, drug addicts, losers were the only voices we heard. There were no agents waiting at the gate to welcome us home. Instead we had to disband our uniforms as a dishonor of our service. No one would come near us as if we returned with a plague. That's beyond peculiarity; just downright disrespectful.

There were no resources available for our care. We were let loose on the unwelcoming streets of America and told you are on your own. That is as sick as sick can be. What mother would send their child off to war and upon his return bearing visible battle wounds and disfiguring scars of pain, disown and forsake the love needed for his healing?

I never chose any war to fight. Those decisions were made for me. When a service is done for honor and country it is to be recognized as such and trumpeted from the highest mountain. I am not one envious of anyone's accomplishment; but on the backs of our sorrow, we have paved the way for those who are currently engaged in war, on their return home, to receive all that is due and rightfully so. If all that's to be concluded of our service, let it be known Vietnam Veterans were warriors abroad and at home; pathfinders clearing a way in the clutter of darkness for others to walk freely in the light.

There is a time for war and there is a time for peace. A time of peace is for healing, regaining one's strength to continue pursuing the freedoms of life. When we have given all that we have to give with the only thing remaining is our dignity and pride, we must allow the oil of joy to return to our lives with the genuineness that only flows from a heart at peace. That my brothers; I truly call *"Exceptional"*.

I offer my sincere gratitude to Martinsburg, WV VA Medical Center, in particular, *"The Hope Center"* for facilitating a transitional environment to our Veterans. PTSD, Agent Orange, Traumatic Brain Injury, Anger Management, Diabetes and a host of cancer related issues due to the consequences of war are serious issues confronting our health professionals and our Nation. With diligence and a strong attitude of acceptance of our service; they continue to render compassionate care to our "Nation's Finest".

Chapter 6

Agents of Rescue

The last to die in Vietnam-Charles McMahon and Darwin Judge were members of the Marine Security Guard (MSG) Battalion at the US Embassy, Saigon and were providing security for the DAO Compound, adjacent to Tân Sơn Nhứt Airport, Saigon. McMahon had arrived in Saigon on 18 April, while Judge had arrived in early March.[3] Both died in a North Vietnamese rocket attack on Tân Sơn Nhứt on the morning of April 29, 1975. (2)

The flame of fire that burns within the heart of every *"Combat Veteran"* is an emancipating gift of courage. Conversely, those same burning flames can be a consuming agent with an annihilating capacity to destroy everything in its path just as the napalm of Vietnam. The synergy of iron fire released from B52 bombers and the raging havoc of flame-throwers combusting in the thickness of the jungle leveled the killing fields. Just as the healing properties of time rehabilitated the mangrove and bamboo trees from such horrifying devastation, so does the heart and soul of the Combat Veteran need the same restitution.

Counselors, doctors and mentors who have spent years in preparation to facilitate the very issues that confront Combat Vets have been put in a precarious situation. They have an enormous task sorting through the benign and sometimes terminal chain of events exclusive to our lives.

As *"Agents of Rescue"*, they mean well in their attempts to scale the rugged crevasses of our mountainous problems in an unconditional path with no prior guidance of a preferred passageway to choose. With ropes and harnesses to secure their own falling, likened to a free style mountain climber scaling a vertical cliff; they make the slow, at times grueling incline to the top to get a better view of what we are contending with. Others make the attempt to burrow their way through in an effort to tap into the core for a sampling to offer remedies for the pain and suffering of the accumulated events of war that are not so easy to dispose.

Drilling through an exterior of hardness is problematic to say the least. Our memories are precious and at times the only recognizable good is intertwined with our disappointments. There is always the risk of relapsing further into the recesses of denial when confronted with truth. Healing is a painful process; from beginning to end, from discovery to acceptance, from responsibility to change; the pathway to recovery dictates that we must consider the cost and not waver in skepticism that tends to grip our reasoning.

For Vietnam Combat Vets, there is a feeling of anesthetic numbness due to nearly 50 years of accumulating calluses which presents itself as a monumental feat for anyone attempting to overcome. Buried deep within our despair, sequestered by the ruggedness of years of layering without resolution, at times we can find answers that have evaded us.

However, unlocking a door without the certainty of a therapeutic solution is a fear we must consider.

The dark mountain of our despair is resistant to any form of illumination shining upon our circumstances. It must be scaled back, stripped of its exterior barriers. We fail to realize our battles are only opportunities for a testimony of a walk of faith. Everyone believes in something; even to the one who says he does not believe, *"Believes in His Unbelief"*. Rays of darkness cannot capture any man turned away from them.

We have built a well fortified defense surrounding our emotions. The protective shield of calloused battle scars we acclaim as an emblem of courage is a disguise of truth. The anguish of suppression of our darkened memories has lasted nearly fifty years and it still seems like it was only yesterday.

Time, patience and the healing oil of love will cut through the resistant powers that held such a grip on our lives; liberating our searching souls with hope. Amazingly, what others have discovered of ourselves, we fail to recognize the treasures buried within us; the riches of gold, silver, platinum, diamonds, and rubies mounted upon a victor's crown of life and freedom.

They can readily see the precious jewels lying dormant within us but the key to unravel the cords that bind us is within our control. It is a decision only we can make. There is a river of life flowing within each one of us that contains a reservoir of hope but our fears are a hindrance which does not easily yield to truth beyond our perceptions.

In defense of our problems, we tend to judge everything operating beneath the visibility of our own failures and if we are not careful, we could become very judgmental of others opinions and perceptions. We have a choice; make our mountain a hiding place masked with trees of denial or we can make the mountain a worship place where there is an endless power of love waiting to embrace us. If we would only look up, we will see *"The Everest of Mountains"* that has been awaiting our recognition. *"Mount Zion"* is its name meaning to be in the Presence of *"The Almighty"* seeking His solutions. It is a name that is familiar to some and new to the skeptic who chooses to live in his own creative existence.

"Without a vision, the people perish." Without eyes to see, we are wandering in darkness. Our solutions are contained within by the choices we make but it is very difficult when our choices are mired in ambiguity. When we look into the mirror, what do we see? Do we see as others see us or do we see ourselves as the only benefactor of truth? Because of the wounds we have been carrying around, the element of trust we've delegated to others is measured to say the least. We're at the crossroads of indecision and it is a great opportunity to allow trusting eyes to see what we cannot see and explore the possibilities lying beneath the veil of our circumstances.

My car has a navigation system which I use quite often. I always know where I am going but don't always know the directions how to get there. I rely so much on the integrity of the system to take me where I need to be but I am not always trusting of the alternate solutions. This is indicative of all of our lives; we can clearly articulate our destiny but don't always know or trust whatever the mechanisms needed to deliver us to our destination.

Vietnam Veterans suffer the same insecurities. The vast majority of us tend to lose focus on our greatest priority; "Trust"! As a principle of faith, I believe; *"Trust is love unsaid. It is confidence mitigated above failure, beyond the thought of our greatest misfortunes. Trust is forbearance liken to a man making a vow to a women; In sickness and in health removing the doubt of suspicion from her insecurities. Trust is verifiable. There is no variance in trust; sees no wrong and can do no wrong."*

The foundation of trust is built upon relationships. I can imagine it is an agonizing process for counselors to develop a conduit that is open and transparent when those bearing the scars of war are reluctant to divulge issues so close to their emotions. I have discovered; our *"secret places"* are not meant for everyone to see, even some whom we have entrusted. There are things pertaining to our identity as Vietnam Vets that are fabricated beyond reasoning; even from those we never would have suspected who gained our confidence, exposing our confidentiality. At times, it is betrayal by the hands of a fellow veteran incensed with retribution because of their inability to cope with their own issues. Failure to communicate amidst turmoil can lead to misunderstandings. It does not take much to disrupt the delicate balance of a psyche that has its roots linked to paranoia.

Many have asked the question of Vietnam Veterans; *"What are the provocations of trust that appear to be so challenging and why does it continue to be such a difficult matter to resolve"?* The answer is very simple; *"Our deepest fears are rooted in distrust. Distrust of our government who lied to us, allowing shame to lay claim upon our sacrifices; disrespect by a population who disowned us below the dignity of valor and honor".*

Our bonds of trust were severed with reproach by an unforgiving society who continues to refuse acceptance of our service. The persistent feeling of contempt runs deep through our veins. We were hurting and nobody cared; no beacon of hope to be found to dispel the darkness surrounding our greatest fears.

The challenges of life are for problem solvers. Some of us are very reluctant to take command over our circumstances but would rather leave the responsibility for someone else to figure out our solutions. Delegating authority is easy but the management of our fears is something only we can do. There are times we muster the courage to move beyond ourselves to trust someone with greater insight but the fear is still there of hearing those harsh and cutting words; *"get over it"*.

I have a deep appreciation for those who have invested in me showing concern and compassion that comes only from the caring. Life is a lifelong learning experience. We can glean from anyone who is delegated with the responsibility and care of participating in our recovery. However, the fear of trust is a difficult task to overcome.

Paradigm of Change

The paradigm of therapeutic care for those who have been dealing with anger, anxiety and depressive disorders has shifted away from just *"only"* pharmaceutical prescriptions by doctors and counselors to that of *"group meetings"*. Group meetings are designed to allow the needed participation and expressions of voices that were heard only in private consultations. Forums have been developed as an interactive exercise tailor-made to the veterans need. In my observation, collaboration of the brotherhood has accelerated the healing process by reshaping synchronizing events that occurred on the battlefield. It has bonded our lives together by redefining the very issues that has kept us apart; separated and isolated from the *"Commonality of our Suffering"*.

Veterans wounded on the battlefield and not just abroad, but also the battles they would experience emerging back into the civilized world, rely so much on the facilitating capabilities of VA's Medical Service Providers. Without them committed to you, your access to available services is limited by the choices someone else is making for you. Needless to say, dealing with a bureaucracy can cause so much stress, strife and discord. Often the wrath that is suffered is to those who only are seeking answers.

There has been an ongoing *"confrontation"* between our Government and Vietnam Veterans going back some forty to fifty years. It has taken this long for them to assume their responsibility to provide the necessary care to our war stricken veterans. In my opinion, it all boils down to a matter of money. We were worthy of the cost of the blood sacrificed but considered not worthy enough for the reward of our suffering. The price for suffering can never be calculated based on percentages and spreadsheets of formulas often used as instruments of denial.

The culture of conspiracy to *"deny, deny and deny*; denial of claims, denial of certifying conditions that can lead to claims until death claims our final denial! We are now seeing this played out in VA Medical Centers as they are being exposed for the world to see how the United States Government has violated the sacred bond of trust committed to taking care of our Wounded Warriors. Some of our veterans lost their lives *"in the free land of America"* by being denied medical care they paid such a dear price to deserve. Ask any veteran how long they have been waiting for services particularly pertaining to expediency adjudicating their claims that have been backlogged for years. Years of waiting on a decision only to be told to wait again.

I must admit that over the years medical treatments at the VA Medical Centers have improved at most facilities for what I've been told. I can see the results through the eyes of electronic media. However, the system is no better than the professionals who opinionate because of their training and biases. There is always the reluctance of validating any medical condition you may have if it does not comply with VA protocol. The protocols are not established to expedite anything in your favor but to frustrate you in the process until you have said; *"I have had enough"*. I know; I have been there as many of you have.

I am very grateful for the Brothers who preceded me. Without their persistence to rectify the injustice of rendering unfettered service to our Vets, we would not be where we are today. I am not being facetious; *"Does this country truly respect our service? Will they ever make amends to keep their promise?*

The Vietnam War ended January 27, 1973. North and South Vietnam, the Viet Cong, and the US signed the Paris Peace Accord on this day, ending one of the longest and most unpopular wars in American history. Despite a ceasefire that had been put into effect a few days earlier, the last American troop to die in Vietnam was killed just 11 hours before the treaty was signed.(5)

Chapter 7

"Fear is a mind killer"

"In the heart of every soldier in wars seen and unseen; wars past and wars to come, the fire must be lit, guarded and protected. Every fire is a source of light, illuminating the pathway of truth, exposing any indifference camouflaged in the secrecy of darkness."

Fear epitomizes the plight of a vast number of veterans that experienced the battlefield. Anxiety which seemingly is the calling card of most Combat Veterans creates the greatest threat to our emotional and mental stability since returning from the warzone. It has plagued our lives during war and continues in some form or fashion to interfere with our progression moving forward. Intrusions of nightmares and paranoia, anger, depression and sociability issues are symptomatic manifestations of the consequences of exposure to the unpredictable nature of war.

The induction of fear in every developing moment in a warzone will condition the hardest of hearts into accepting the vulnerabilities of the unknown. Fear is a challenge to anyone's confidence when surrounded by uncertainties. Ultimately, it will deplete your strength to reason effectively and function with a sense of normalcy concerning one's survival. Being truthful, my initial response upon my arrival in Vietnam without any other attributing factor was the fear of dying and returning home in a box.

Fight-Flight-Fright

The first lesson I learnt after arriving in the warzone was fight or flight. These were elective choices; the courage to take a stance and fight or with the same energy, flee in fear. During my time in the jungle, I never witnessed anyone who was fearful to the extent of fleeing but some did as I did; I became paralyzed with *"fright"*. That was an easy lesson I would learn after only my third day of arriving in-country.

During my first firefight, I was equipped with all of the armor needed to defend myself; an M16 Assault Rifle and two bandoliers of ammo to ward off any intrusion. As one could not have imagined, the disarming effect of fright came upon me over-riding control of my responsiveness. I was petrified! I dropped my weapon and clutched the trunk of a bamboo tree as if to hide my fear. If the tree could have bled, it would have hemorrhaged from the clutch of death I had around its trunk.

The consolidation of fear had driven me to point of incoherency. The only thing I heard after the smoke settled was a voice blasting in my ear; *"It's over, it's over as one of the Brothers pried my hands from around the tree"!* What an embarrassing betrayal of my senses? I vividly remember the

Brothers laughing at me hysterically as if they were saying; *"Welcome to Vietnam!"* I had officially become one of them. I never would have thought of the day I could be as blind as a groundhog in search of his shadow or deaf as prey trying to elude the stealth of an eagle. I was speechless with the muted tongue of fear. What a dreadful introduction into the suddenness of the unexpected. It set the framework for the battles that would follow but I would recover.

Pump the Brakes

Fright is a terror that will ravish your mind robbing you of your sensibilities. The suddenness of unregulated fear can exceed its boundaries by overwhelming your senses rendering you in a powerless state. It short circuits your ability to make rational decisions, leaving you frozen in a gasp of suspension. It is not an indictment of the lack of courage as some would suggest even though trepidation from exploding rockets and rapidity of gun fire coming our way did act as an accelerant propelling my emotions into unfamiliar places.

The syndrome of fright was a prelude for times that would come and go in what I have determined to be panic attacks. It is rather amazing the things that are so routine can come to a screeching halt when we are overwhelmed by a sudden and invasive episode of fear, gripping our emotions with the worst case of dread imaginable. The unwanted intrusions that trigger panic have never left me. They have developed into a life of their own.

I have discovered panic is spontaneous more so than generalized fear. The parameters of fear can be controlled by the places you go, people that you see, sounds, smells and recall of places you've been. As a solution, many veterans choose the path of avoidance but the evading process can lead to different issues further down the road.

The spontaneity of panic is a fear within itself. It puts you in a state where you have lost all control and your instinct to survive is weakened in a maze of confusion. During a panic attack you will experience a freezing effect with a high level of sensitivity to paranoia because of an imbalance of hormonal distribution controlled by your adrenal glands. An out of balanced hormonal distribution can be the catalyst for indiscriminate responses when our emotions are driven into frenzy. It can be mistakenly identified as a lack of courage. Courage precedes fear and is the anthem of every soldier engaged in war. However, when courage faces unknown possibilities *(Trojan Horse of fear)*, it is never a given what the outcome will be.

A soldier's DNA is not attached to the dog tags hanging around his neck or the oath he takes but is in the blood he bleeds. Every soldier who has lost his life on the battlefield, memories and a pleated flag given to the love ones of the fallen are the only things remaining of a life he once lived. Besides a love that is separated forever void of an opportunity of expression, a soldier's grave has no voice to speak neither does it have ears of interpretation but it does echo a resounding cry for reattachment to love and peace.

In Vietnam, I encountered the John Waynes and Rambos. They were the reckless ones *(gung ho)* that had no fear. Seemingly you would think so but lifting the veil beneath their countenance you would see the source of their protected fear; weed, cocaine, opium, heroin and alcohol. Being frank with you, some were just flat out crazy with no fear of dying.

I made the decision to join the fight for myself and those around me rather than to surrender in regret. Subsequently, I incorporated a vice into my life that haunted me years after my return home to the States. It turned into a lifestyle worthy of the consequences it produced. It was the choice of drugs I used as a pacifying agent to calm my fears and disillusionment of memories I tried so hard to forget. Every human being exists with the same intangibles as another. Given the circumstances, who is to say what your choice would be?

For years I struggled in the wilderness suffering, wanting to be free but could never find the answers that were right in front of me. Everything I touched turned to failure; relationships, jobs and the failed attempt to finish my education. I could readily see where this road would end. It appeared that everyone on the planet did not understand me. They had me stigmatized as the crazy one without recognizing where I had been. I had become the black sheep who had failed in honor not deserving of life's second chance. The keys to my future had been thrown amongst the ruins of discovery seemingly without the hope of reclaiming.

There truly is no conception of war except the ones that fight it! The images portrayed on television will never serve justice to the embattled souls who risked all for the sake of duty. War is not sensational but brutal with no conscience of compassion. The life of a soldier should not be minimized and his/her devoted effort should be viewed with the greatest honor and respect.

The only way to truly know the toil it takes on one's life is to have been there; that is everyone except my Mother. She never lost her faith in me and constantly gave me a diet of encouragement and love. A mother's love is irreplaceable and burns with flames of an eternal fire even when the smothered vapors from the candle of life cease. Despite the years of separation, my Mother's maternal instincts are ever so present outreaching with a love that continues to brood as from the day of my beginnings.

Even though years have passed since I last embraced her, there is a longing that yet remains in my spirit. In my transparency, if I expressed out of my heart from the reservoir of my weeping, you would weep with me. It is a mountain void of fulfillment but the joy remains born from memories of love and affection that give me comfort as I embrace my own mortality that awaits me.

Part II

"Secret Battles"

Women did not serve in the same military capacity as they do now. There were approximately 7,484 female nurses who served in Vietnam, which was the only military assignment that they were allowed to participate. Since there were only 8 female nurses who died, the information on the nurses is featured in greater detail. (6)

Sankofa

"Sankofa" symbolizes a mythic bird that flies forward while looking backward with an egg symbolic of the future in its mouth. It bears the seeds to repaint the patterns of our dreams and visions deferred from yesterday's sorrows with the hope of tomorrow's fulfillment. Our future is embodied in our past laden with the sufferings from generations that sacrificed in faith. It is an investment not so easily recognized amidst the changing winds blowing from centuries past.

"Sankofa" teaches that we must go back to our roots, the place of our beginnings, reaching back to discover the best of what our past has to teach us. In order to achieve our full potential as we move forward, we must never forget the sacrifices of our Elders.

The pathway of our destiny to recover whatever we have lost, forgotten, forgone or been stripped of can be reclaimed, revived, preserved and perpetuated for our future. Time is a filter; a discriminate judge of the choices we make. It is given to us as a gift born from the revelation of God's creativity.

KOFI'S VIEW

"A Prelude into the Secrecy of Hidden Fire"
(Invitation Only!)

Kofi is a name I acquired in Ghana, West Africa. It simply means *"Friday Born"*. Part of the Ghanaians' naming convention incorporates the day of the week you were born as part of your legal name. I was born on a Friday, not in a hospital, but with the assistance of midwives in my parent's home.

The Ghanaians are very peaceful, living in the confines of a secured democracy. Their history dates back to beginnings I never knew and they are quick to give a narration of their development as a Nation dating back centuries upon centuries. They are predominately a Christian Nation but live within the tolerance to accommodate anyone's belief.

Ghana is a country of enormous wealth to include newly discovered oil off its shores. They have emerged as a prominent influence amongst the African Nations. Although they have adopted western ways, they still continue to practice their native traditions. Every Friday, on the day of

"Kofi"; everyone wears their cultural clothing as a symbol of allegiance and unanimity; honoring their past with sacred respect for their Elders.

While in Ghana, I was bestowed with the honor of an "*Ashanti Chief*" recognizing me as *"Chief Sankofa"*. That was a special moment even though I have ambivalent feelings concerning the reason of my ascension into a place I had never considered. I now had a kingdom with the responsibility of subjects needing my leadership and financial support. I did not readily consider the cost. I was put into shoes too large for me but *"It left enough room for my feet to grow into"*.

Years have passed since I last sat in my *"Chief's Seat"*; my feet haven't grown and my kingdom is nowhere to be found. Later I would realize the proverbial wisdom of the Elders: *"What good is a king without a kingdom"?* Let it be known to all; *"I've been where others never will go; I've seen what they never will see and I've done what they never will do"*. Though disappointments have followed me, my future remains resilient because I still control the *"keys"* to unlock any door; even the key back into my kingdom!

Reflections of My Elders

Looking back through the periscope of time of my early days being raised in the South, what stood out to me and still continues to be part of my fabric are those times I spent in the Church. I went so much, it seemed like it was my second home. Whatever the occasion, it was no doubt there would be a pew waiting for me. Outside of the Church, there was nothing to do except taking care of the chores of an enormous farm. Mules, cows, chickens, pigs and of course those pesky guinea fowl demanded continual care. There were so many snakes crawling around it seemed as if we were raising them too. I tried my best to kill every one of them I saw.

I have a vivid memory of the testimonies of the Saints as they gathered in the Sanctuary. They were *"Soldiers"* not from a horizontal plane but vertically connected. Once a year, they had their Annual Revival Services that continued throughout the week. It was a time when families from the surrounding community would gather in hope; waiting for the promise of a better day.

I still remember the resounding thunder of foot stomping echoing on wooden floors and hands clapping in a rhythm of celebration for the seeking souls bowed in surrender; some waiting on bended knee while others were prostrated waiting at the waters of invitation for the inevitable power of The Almighty to fall.

The exhibition of shouts of joy and even their tears still resonate within the inner recesses of my conscience. In my quiet moments of reflections, I am often reminded of their confessions of faith. Though many years have come and gone, I still remain connected to their burdens and sorrows born of poverty as they struggled to breakthrough an oppressive environment that had them bound because of the color of their skin. The sanctuary of the Church provided a safe haven away from the toils and confrontations of living in the shadow of another man's dominion.

To know a servant you must have been a servant. Empathic gestures from those who never experienced such humiliation will never fully embrace the concept of what it means to have been denied without acceptance of the history that produced it. Even a servant has dreams of a better life with the same amenities afforded every civil minded human being. It is one thing to serve another but it is much better to acquire the freedom to exercise one's individual choices.

At week's end of revival, the atmosphere was charged with a sense of empowerment and a renewal of strength to continue. The weariness of their struggles gave way to the possibilities of faith that was echoed in songs of victory. After the battle and a moment basking in triumphal celebration, their struggles continued; the agony of perseverance returned. There is never an end to the battle of faith. The greater reward is to the resolute who endure until the end without wavering in unbelief.

Every human being is endowed with the power of faith. Everybody believes in something for without it, the success of life is impossible to achieve. I never doubted the faith of my Elders, however, the weariness of time settled in and they retreated from the concourse of war surrendering to the greater challenges that confronted them. I remember hearing songs of resignation that contended with their faith echoing a reversal of their convictions as they waited for a new generation to emerge. A generation wiser and bolder embracing the gains accomplished through the sufferings of the past.

We are resilient in our victories but there are times new conflicts will emerge gravitating in dimensions that can be so overwhelming. Every war; every battle potentially can make you weary and drain you of strength. With a journey ended, the unbelieving pursues the beaten path, an unsecured path of retreat blazing a trail away from the beacon of faith.

Subsequently, my Elders retired their weapons. The battle remaining exceeded the limits of where their faith had settled. The consequences of living a life riddled in poverty morphed into greater challenges as the years relinquished any success not required as a necessity for living. Poverty has its ambition. Despite the fleeting moments of aspirations in response to unfulfilled dreams, the variable winds of change are not easily apprehended. While fleeing with their dreams in shambles, they confessed in resignation:

> *"Why should we sacrifice more than we've already given? We have fought every battle to be fought. Our battles never end. They come with the swiftness of spiraling fear, there is no other resolve other than to surrender." Just as a grasshopper trapped in the wild winds of fire and as a violin played on muted strings, they resign with the song of their harp tuned to the beat of a drum inviting the winds of change. The baton is passed on to a generation who will not bend or brake."*

With no strength remaining and a will to continue, they succumb, denying the greater power of faith. They search for the valley of peace as they await the destiny of the unknown; somewhere listening for their name. It is a journey ended with no more battles to be fought. They have fought the good fight of faith and discharged their mantle casting it into the winds of change.

In my preparations, I have been waiting for this moment of greatness to emerge. With the speed of a gazelle and the boldness of a lion king, I apprehended the mantle cast in the winds of faith. I hear a voice speaking from afar hiding in the discovery of my destiny, *"Why did you come down here"*? I pondered, searching deep within me, exploring every corridor of my being; trembling as clashing cymbals resonating into the higher dimensions of my mind searching for an answer. With boldness I mount up the courage and answered; *"What have I done now? Is there not a cause?"* Then a power of strength emerged within me with the voice of faith and spoke to the gainsayers shrouded in fear;

> *"I came because I believe." I believe in the secrecy of my preparations where my faith was proven. The bigger the battle I discovered the greater the victory. I've encountered the bear and the lion as a protector of the weak and feeble. I provided strength to the faint, food to the hungry and water to the thirsty. For every threatening voice that says I can't: I will"*.

In the silence of hiding while I waited patiently for the opportunities of faith to emerge, I prepared for the victory. I discovered the secret of my battle, *"The battle is not mine but it is The Almighty's battle; The Defender of justice and equality"*. The champion of my adversary is a giant awaiting me but he does not know the champion of my faith. Through the eyes of man, I am a dead man walking in the presence of overwhelming strength but I know the power of God's gifts that will sustain me in His grace.

For forty days morning and evening, the enemy brought fear and shook the foundation of belief in the heart of the fearful. They fled in fear and were dreadfully afraid. From the wilderness I came shrouded in faith with my weapons tried in the honing fires of a blazing furnace. I stood upon the pedestal of faith, searching the valley below, waiting to see the champion who had caused so much fear. I was challenged by echoing words of defeat. Did they not know that *"I came for such a time as this"*?

I stood in power amongst the fearful whose faith was proven weaker than my foe. I answered their threatening;

"Is there not a cause"?

The cause of faith was proven in the wilderness when I struck the lion and the bear and delivered the lamb from its mouth. I caught it by its beard, struck and killed it. In the valley of decisions, I discovered the power of The Almighty that humbled my pride. In the battles that were greater than my ability to master, I discovered faith in hiding and power in believing. I hastened with accelerated power and ran toward the battle and not in retreat. The courage of a *"Soldiers"* heart will never surrender but will always endure to the end!

"Faith is a horizontal display of heaven's smile"

Chapter 8

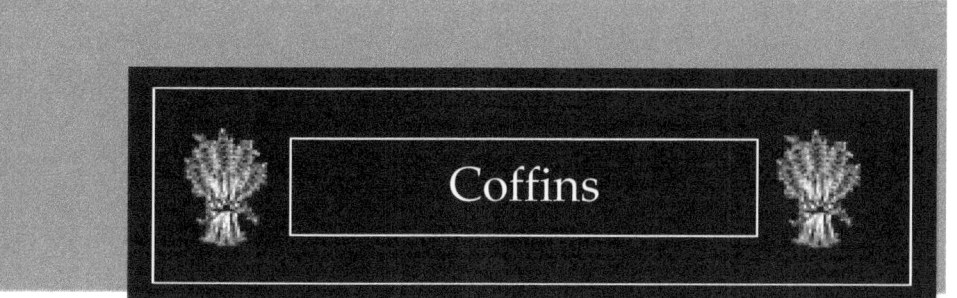

Designated after the new time frame authorized by Congress, Frank Huddleston, US Army who was 68 years old (16E, 109) died in the United States. (4)

In one of my night seasons I had a dreadful vision. To some, it was a vision, to others it was a nightmare. Either way, it was very profound. I refer to a vision as living lucidly in the moment of your dream. As for a nightmare, the jungles of Vietnam permanently scarred my conscience with a signature of regret. In my sleeping moments which I call seasons, I never know where my dreams will take me. I could be on the mountain top to see where a new day will take me or in the torrid rapids below struggling in turmoil to break free from haunting memories of days gone by.

The war in Vietnam served its purpose to rob me of life; stealing my dreams and the joys of friendship by supplanting seeds of doubt and destruction. It distorted my personality from one who had embraced love as a principle influence to becoming antagonistic; living with a conscience flooded with hostile memories.

In my vision, I was standing by the side of the road at a bus stop waiting with a *"coffin"* under my arm. Let me ask you; does that seem unusual? Why in tarnation would somebody carry around a coffin everywhere they went?

When the bus arrived, I tried with awkwardness to get on but I needed help. It was too heavy for me to carry by myself. The bus driver moved everyone to the rear of the bus to make room for my displacement. He grabbed one end of the coffin and I had the other. Somehow we managed to squeeze it through the door. We placed it in the center of the isle which created a major impediment and caused massive confusion. Nobody could get on and nobody could get off. It was so big that it took up half the space on the bus.

With desperation written upon my face, I noticed the attitude of the people as they looked at me with distain. The driver of the bus was annoyed as he stared at me through his rear view mirror. Frankly speaking, he was tired of helping me with my problem and the people did not appreciate being inconvenienced to accommodate me and my coffin.

As I looked out of the window, I saw a funeral procession going by on the way to the cemetery. It was the funeral of one of our fallen soldiers who had died on the battlefield. The processions haven't ended; the parade of flags draping unresponsive coffins continues on the road of no return. My spirit continues to cry out; *"when will it end"*?

I awoke troubled in my spirit searching for the meaning of the vision in my head. I knew God was speaking but what exactly was He saying. After much pondering, truth emerged and I began to see myself as others had seen me.

It is not a normal process to be carrying around a coffin everywhere you go as if I didn't know. Standing at a bus stop with a coffin under my arm is out of the ordinary. Obviously what I was carrying around had become highly visible to everyone, so big that I could not hide it any longer.

I had no idea the compromising imposition I subjected others to. I was living in my own deception. Without knowing, submission to the influence of deceptive behavior had gained dominance over my character and integrity. For all the presumptive good that I would do, seemingly it always produced a counter result.

As Combat Veterans, we've all had problems of past encounters that have affected the lives of many, even those we loved the most; our wives, children, families and even our friends. Seemingly, we have a tendency to push them away, denying the good of their intentions. The humility of accommodating others into our lives at times seems remote if not impossible. It's all because of fear.

The coffin represented dead things; mountains of despair that happened in my life that I had no power to change. For some reason I could not and would not separate myself from yesterday's experience of my failures. *"There is a time and season for everything under the sun"*, but when the time has come and gone to release unnecessary burdens imposed upon us, we would have missed a valuable opportunity that could have accelerated our liberation. Subsequently, procrastination of addressing issues so close to our emotions has a tendency to create greater problems at a time when we so desperately need to bring order into our affairs.

When we fail to conquer, we compound past issues relative to our healing. If we continue reliving negativity borne from our experiences over and over again and not let go, we are setting ourselves up for defeat. The thoughts of defeat will occupy our destiny and alter the path before us. Ultimately because of our inability to move beyond the threshold of smoking mirrors, depression will settle in and have us fixated on our misery. Below the surface of our discontent, anxiety will be lurking at our door to exacerbate any attempt to escape.

The spiritual connection of grief to the brokenness of love deeply rooted in our spirit has no other comparison. It is an undeniable force which indicates that we have lost something or someone very close to us. Grief is a perfectly legitimate part of our human nature but it is a strong force that can be overwhelming when we don't factor in the time it takes to recover. Prolonged grieving opens the door to the temptation of depression. It can happen as a result of being too close to the intensity of our suffering. When depression settles in, it further embattles our ability to maintain the balance of our emotional state.

The process of grieving is purposed to bring reparation to our lives from so much despair and brokenness. I have discovered, as a War Veteran, the battlefield does not afford the opportunity to grieve. So we do the next best thing; the only thing; *"We Weep"*. It is very difficult to carry something so close to the vest without being afforded the opportunity to expunge our emotional attachments through the natural order it was meant to be. To alter the connection between our emotions and thinking is very troubling to say the least. Somewhere down the line, reality will set in and we will be faced with the consequence of having deferred the verdict of our emotions which may have taken years to resurface. Searching for the root cause of our troubles amidst scattered memories we choose to forget requires a level of transparency and true recollection of events that were delayed since our tenure in the jungle.

We have a tendency to compartmentalize our emotions without bringing to the surface our true feelings. The more we suppress the more miserable we become. We should not allow what's purposed for today to be carried over into another season. *"Deal with it!"* There is nothing good we will accomplish by circumventing decisions that are crucial to our emotional stability. Again I say; *"Deal with it!"* Time is of the essence! You have heard the saying *"I will serve no wine before its time"*. The ending of one season must be ripened and complete for power to enter into the next without the liability of *"living for today locked into memories of the past"*.

Depression is the seed of denial. Depression simply means *"I shoulda, woulda, coulda"*. Acceptance of truth beyond our ability to change must somehow be adequately dealt with and put into proper perspective. We all have a tendency to codify the heaviness that comes upon us but usually it results in unequal distribution leaving our emotional state fragmented. Just as the coffin was too heavy for me to bear, it would have been easier if I did not have to carry it at all.

There is a place for dead things and we all have been there. It is called the cemetery. It is a place where people and at times, memories of a defeated past are laid to rest. It is a place of final acceptance beyond our ability to change. By the way, you and I already have advanced reservations. Even though our time of check in maybe later than others; believe me, at some point in our journey forward, we will check into those *"Residential Gardens"*. They will always have enough room. Every day of our lives, there are things that surface from our past but we must get on with the business of living for today. Being honest, it is not always easy as it may sound.

There were years that slipped by me when I returned from Vietnam. Inability to muster the courage needed to resolve bygone issues haunted me much further down the road than I had expected. Today is a new day; a day I never lived before. But yesterday is still there with memories that do not lend its truth of what tomorrow will be. One thing for sure, I will live for today with all intentions of fulfilling every moment to reclaim what yesterday did not produce.

Chapter 9

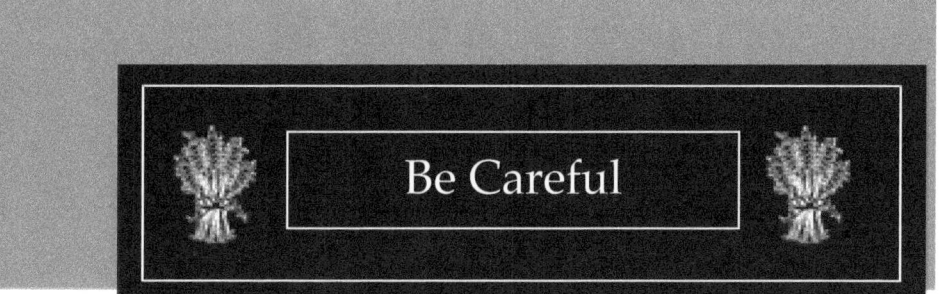

It was on a Friday I last visited my Mother in the hospital. She had been fighting the good fight of faith to overcome a disease that laid claim to her future. As we sat by her bedside, she told us of her decision. She had decided her fate for a greater hope. It was the promise of faith endowed with the hope of continuance; *"Faith in the resurrection"*. It is a hope that we all will have to consider before our journey ends; the choice to relinquish the temporary occupation of this tabernacle of flesh for the living promise of eternal life. My Mother, being the spiritual woman she was, made a statement of faith and decided that she had done all she could do and had no regrets of unfinished work. She told us:

> *"I have no regrets but if there is one, it would be that if there was any good that I could have done that I did not do, for that I regret."*

Her work had finished. She told us that life without health is not worth the investment of faith. Our gifts separated from our strength are reflective of a journey ending its continuance, removing power from the works of our hands. With nothing left to connect to this life, the greater destiny of an eternal hope awaits the promise of a never ending life; a life of transformation from the weakness of the flesh and the frailties of a conscience not willing to yield to time's inevitability of invisible spiritual life. To the Believer, even in death, our work is not finished for we die in hope of the promise of a new world that will emerge out of the preparation of God's faithfulness.

It has always amazed me to see those who believe they came from nothing and will return to nothing. There was always something from the beginning of time that made a determination of our existence. I don't know the truth of beginnings pertaining to the evolving nature of our world; I wasn't there and neither were you but I choose to believe I have always been and will always be.

As I am sitting here pondering over my thoughts, two days before my birthday, I am taken back to the day of my entombment in my Mother's womb. I can feel the pains of birth, the travail of nine months encased in the nourishing waters of life. With her blood flowing through me, enriched in hope, waiting for the final hour of delivery, I can imagine her excitement surfacing beyond the pain.

It is rather amazing as I calculate the time she gave of her life carrying me and my siblings in her womb. For the seven of us, 63 months of her 76 years were devoted to childbirth.

The love she gave raising us was unique and unconditional to each one of us. Our lives will never exceed the boundaries of her giving, but collectively the greater value of her contributions will forever remain as a testimony for generations to come.

Surrendering in Hope

With our lives surrendered and destiny completed, the call of faith yearns for something greater than the life we've experienced. It is the wings of love waiting to embrace us, to complete us, making us into an image with no material boundaries. The Almighty's immortality intercepts at junctions end of our mortality with penetrating light shining upon our garments separating soul and spirit. At the beginning of life we adorned a soul with the breath of life that does not cease until our day of ceasing. At the end of our journey, our gifts are recalled and we return the breath with our soul rested, surrendered in peace.

The wisdom of Biblical scripture reveals we are to honor God with our youth while we have the health and energy to perfect the vision of life. With no more life to give, our choices become clear;

> *"To be absent from a body weakened in strength is to embrace a far greater hope in the promise of something greater than the life we've lived."*

When years have turned our hair to silver and we begin to flirt with eternity with no more wicks to trim the dimming of our lamps, the curtain draws to a close. Mother told us to take her home. No more transfusions, no more blood, no more needles and no more suffering. She embraced the Cross as hope of a continual life in the Spirit. Her parting words to me were the words of an angel whose time had come to reclaim the everlasting peace in the Presence of the King. With a smile still lingering upon her countenance she said; *"You are going to miss me when I am gone"*. Little did I realize the power of her words and how quickly they would testify! After a couple of days at home, from her bedside she spoke her last words to me. Whispering in softness and sincerity of love, she said;

"Be Careful"

How swiftly the angels were summoned for her escort. They came with the swiftness of my tears. I struggled with the pain of my emotions to grasp the reality of my world in turmoil. The flame of love burnt through the hardness of my conscience and I wept as the wailings of Jesus at Gethsemane and the agony of pain He suffered on the cross. I felt like a lion king who had lost its pride only to wander in the wilderness of despair. My cry was a cry of forsaken love that ran so deep in my veins. How I longed for the love that had enriched my life with hope, a hope that I must now live alone. It is a lonely life of justice ordered by the sequencing of time that can't be recalled.

My Mother and I had a very special relationship. Without a doubt, she was the catalyst that saved my life from no hope to an inspired possibility that I could recover from the wounds of war. She was the guardian of my destiny; a bridge over troubled waters that led me to that place to discover who I truly was. When I had lost all belief in myself, she nourished me back to life, resuscitating my mind, body and spirit regaining the strength of self-esteem. The purity of her love was an inspiration replacing the hatred that had settled in my heart from my days in Vietnam. To be true, I had become no greater than the people who hated me. Hatred is blinding and is the worst form of ugliness any human being can experience. *"It will destroy you"!*

Learning to Smile All Over Again

Life has a humor but at times it is difficult to find. This I would discover when my Mother separated from this life. In humor there is a convenience to camouflage our tears. Buried behind the veil of laughter is where I masked years of pain hidden from the world to see. How I longed for the rain to shroud the agony that descended upon me. The pain of pretentious smiles had no longevity. The effort to rearrange its unnatural appearance was as a chameleon camouflaging its colors; hiding beneath a masquerade of fear.

Pain is easy to discern by the truth emerging from our smiles. True smiles are connected to the instance of joy surfacing from the passion of our inner feelings. It is an expression of freedom just as a candle of light illuminates our heartfelt emotions. The release of joy is genuine; ever so transparent and is only limited by our expressions. I discovered that the pain of grief also is a transparent truth, translucent as a jellyfish with tentacles searching deep into corridors hidden behind a protective shield. Grief is a protected place where not just any and everyone can enter. It is by invitation only to access the treasures buried beneath our vulnerabilities.

I also discovered that despair has transforming power. It separates the power of love from our hope leaving a deep passion yearning for fulfillment. Saying goodbye is not always the easiest thing to do. It can seem as surreal as a never ending dream. I still struggle from grief of my friends lost in Vietnam but the greater grief of maternal separation looms heavier within me.

I finally got to the place of accepting my Mother's passing; moving away from denial towards acceptance of a truth I wanted so desperately to change. It was an agonizing endeavor not realizing where my pursuits would take me. I searched endlessly through perpetual tears, searching to recapture the boldness of faith for the unfinished destiny awaiting me. My heart ached seemingly without end from conflicting sorrow that continued to brew in my emotions.

Ultimately, humility began to rest upon the mantle of my understanding. Bellows of smoke fumed from my heart dissipating with the fragrance of separation as of a dying lily. The journey forward would follow the path of faith to encounter the healing streams that brought solace to my despair. I decided I would embrace love renewed in the power of God's Spirit with a triumphant praise over my defeats.

Through our journey, the hands of love of the Comforter of Peace brings comfort to our struggles to fulfill the meaning of our existence. He brings to the surface all of our gifts, even our fears in defense of faith when our hope wanes in despair. Hope is the fuel of our existence, without it there would be no life to live. At the beginning of birth, we are commissioned to live out our years beyond the hope of surrender until its completed end. It is an insurmountable captivity without the chance of escaping if you remain faithful and cherish every breath life renders unto you.

At the crossroads of the life's conclusion, we may consider that it is better to continue our journey embracing the unknown rather than linger living a life of depleted strength, diminished in our ability to exercise our will. But I am resolved in faith knowing that the greater reward of my unfinished work awaits me.

The Mind of a Child

In an unprovoked moment while taking my Grandson to Kindergarten, he made a profound statement of how he views the world.

"God is mad and Jesus is really upset!" Why Son? *"Because people are killing other people. What's that guy name down below?"* His name is Satan. *"Oh yea; he is really really mad!"* Why Son? *"Because God is giving him too many people!"*

Var'Shae Barnes (5 years old)

Chapter 10

The only evacuation from the American Embassy took place at the end of April 1975. Frequent Wind was the code name for the evacuation plan. On the Armed Forces Radio station, "White Christmas" was played. The last flight out was at 7:53 pm on April 30, 1975. **(9)**

Liken to pillars of fire and fiery missiles from the glowing breath of mountains, our tears fall upon the ground never to return. They could be as torrential as the monsoon rains of Vietnam or delicate as the evaporating mist of an April shower. They separate from us as emotional grief in search of an occupant to fill the void only to find no substitute for their cause. If it wasn't for our tears, we would not know our laughter from our sorrow. We weep when our joy turns to sorrow and we weep when we have overcome life's misfortune turning our sorrows into joy. Our tears are an indication of the richness that flows from the power center of our affections as the passion of time separates our victories from our misgivings.

It's impossible to reclaim our tears; they never return; lost forever as a forgotten cause worthy of expenditure. The deep cleansing power of those salty drippings of desperation exercise as a free will of the heart yearning for love and things we cherish which are alienated from us. Conversely, when our hearts are overwhelmed with the passion of peace and love, joy emerges as welcomed contentment. Then our hearts will flood, pulsating with an exuberating display of tears repainting the impressions of love.

Tears purify our conscience in the salty waters of despair. Rolling downward upon our cheeks, they stream as a river of life dwelling within us, trickling to a drop until our soul becomes empty. They create a sea of forgetfulness that purge our hearts from fear and despair restoring our countenance with a radiant glow that only love can provide.

When our tears have finished, there is a peace that settles within with a reverence of hope and strength to engage the battles ahead. Just as a pressure cooker vents with whistling steam, so will the torrid of our emotions eventually settle and the rhythm of our hearts will no longer race in fear. Descending from heated desperation to calming waters reflecting as a mirror of peace, the time will come when we must remove the lid that held us together and we will find the completion of a process ready to continue negotiating the trials of living. With restored equilibrium, tears of joy brings restoration to the fragments of hopelessness that had such a gripping affect on our emotional stability but with the caveat; *"The challenges of life will never end and neither will our tears"*.

Our tears are not just simply tears. There is a process and purpose for their formation. They form as a mixture of salt to protect our eyes. When we weep, saline solution excretes from the ducts of our eyelids leaving a trail of salt stains upon our cheeks and can be retraced to the source of our triggered emotions. At times the vision of our eye can lead us down an unwanted path that can result in great humiliation. Subsequently, we will bring tears upon ourselves by our indiscrete decisions. When gullibility exceeds our reasoning, that is to say biting off more than we can chew; then we choke in *"un-rhythmic"* sounds of desperation, sobbing in despair. We can eliminate most heartaches and anguish we face if we would apprehend the mantle of patience needed in our cognitive decisions.

The circumstances of life are very unpredictable and cannot be scripted what a new day will bring. Today we could be on the mountain top but tomorrow we could have fallen in the valley below. When our faith has lost its ability to recover, the saving power of tears will bring humility upon us; clearing our sight as sparkles of light. It is then gladness appears as a welcomed embrace waiting the transition of a season's end. Gladness dispels the insecurities from our past and silences the tears that have dampen the fire of our spirit.

When I left the shores of Vietnam, the fire of my spirit needed rekindling but I didn't have the spark to reignite my passion so diminished in the recesses of failure. I have to express in truth how glad I am that I made it out alive even though time was never given to my recovery. Looking through the rear view mirror of the looking glass, I see the trails of mountains and valleys only to recognize that they are my own. But looking ahead I see a beacon with a torch of light shining upon my destiny.

Weeping

Weeping is a universal language common to all human beings which needs no translation or interpretation to comprehend. Even animals have feelings capable of weeping from desperation to retrieve their lost or from disrespect of the value of our treatment of them. They are an integral part of God's universal order and definitely have a purpose just as we do in maintaining the balance of creation. Birds, bees and all flying things still pollinate our flowers and crops; fish still continue to provide us with food and the lion still continues to wean the weak and feeble from being passed on into our food chain.

It is very disheartening to see how we have plundered the Earth, the place of our residency, as if there is no recourse for our actions. The Earth weeps as we do, turning fumes of pollution into avenging storms, tornadoes and hurricanes as we have never seen before. Even earthquakes bellowing from the deep fail to get our attention of the atmospheric change surrounding our existence. Our icecaps are melting and ocean level rising shifting the balance of the Earth's axis and we still remain in denial when the evidence is right before us.

It is very difficult to hide our emotions when they begin to sway in a sea of uncertainties. Emotional turmoil can shift its balance and the salty drippings will flow until our cup becomes full and nonreturnable. Weeping is an indication of our equilibrium being out of balance with the scales tilted in the direction away from our emotional center.

Weeping has a spiritual component attached to our human existence purposed to cleanse the recesses of our soul and spirit. When we release our fears and doubts, a spring spouting seeds of hope reserved for our liberation will replenish the vacancy left from our sufferings and tears. It is like a river separating one season of our lives to enjoy freedom to enter into the next. Anticipating hope of a new day will refresh our countenance just as the showers of spring falling upon the seeds of winter will burst with the fragrance of blossoms filling the air.

The world is weeping; crying for peace; searching deep into every aspect of our existence to find a place of solace. Wars raging solely for the purpose of man's quest for dominance and superiority of ideas only reflect his insecurities and moral weakness of his human nature. Violence, hatred, famine, poverty but most importantly, *"Unforgiveness"* is an earmark of his failed ideology. The Earth needs no more giving of our blood; we have given enough but yet we still insist that more is not enough.

Unforgiveness is the lost compassion of love with a heart hardened beyond the point of weeping. At the root of unforgiveness lie the imperfections of love that has shackled man's heart, keeping him occupied with vindication and misery of his choices. The pathway to liberation is open, but he refuses to acknowledge his humility, substituting pride as justifiable means *"exceptional to his thinking"*.

The lack of humility is an exaltation of pride. Pride is a vehicle that will compromise any man and crumble him into great despair. Buried with the stress of material burdens and his wayward self-righteousness, man has carved a path into a trench for his own demise. Little does he know, the trench he has dug for others, he has dug for himself. Succumbed to greed by depriving the poor, he has sealed his fate with a disaster waiting to happen with only misery as his company.

The seasonal moments of weeping are not made to last forever. At some point in negotiating the trials of life, we must recognize that weeping is *"just"* a transitional state, a birthing place from one state to another. Life is filled with opportunity to produce something greater than where our expectations have settled but with certainty, we must make the effort despite where yesterday's disappointments may have taken us.

At the beginning of each day, there is always the morning dew that awaits the glow from the rising sun to transform darkness into light, weakness into strength, sorrow into joy, despair into hope and unforgiveness into a heart of compassion. Set your face to greet the rising sun embracing the possibilities of what a new day will bring.

> *"I would rather be shaped by my failures than to never have failed at all."*

Chapter 11

Five Seconds to Midnight

Smith is represented by 667 veterans. (10)

During the course of this writing, My Father separated from this life for the greater promise of hope; hope in the everlasting provisions of the promise of faith. I am honored to have been with him in those fleeting moments of life's betrayal as he crossed over the barrier of time into the unknown dimensions of time and eternity. I had discerned the season and time of his remaining days and embraced the commitment of his love and devotion shared in the lives of so many that he touched. When the Angels of God were summoned riding upon the Chariot Wings of Destiny to escort this *"Servant of Faith"* into the promise, he left no unfinished work.

He was a man of principle and fearless with the boldness of a lion's heart but humbled as a servant of peace. He stood as a monument of courage with intestinal fortitude that never surrendered; always believing in the creative power of faith that transcends all natural boundaries.

He did not have the opportunity to pursue his education as so many of us have which some seem to squander but like many of his generation born in the poverty of the South, he was ushered into the responsibility of being a *"Man-Child"* before his season. What he did not learn in secular institutions, he excelled beyond the restrictions of poverty and disparity and entered the *"School of Faith"*. Where others stopped at the chalk boards of intellectualism, he pursued a life of prosperity woven in faith.

He was a spiritual man; a king sanctioned from Heaven above who walked in authority amongst men. His belief and convictions, truly, produced the provisions for my success. I am very thankful for the example of his life with submission of true gratitude for the unconditional power of his love that I will embrace throughout eternity.

My father trail blazed a path for my future with cemented steps for me to follow. My heart weeps embracing his sacrifices as he laid down his life as a seed of hope for his generation. I will always maintain the connection to the place of his sufferings, never surrendering in forgetfulness the testimonies, sacrifices and wisdom he discovered while travailing in a fallowed path I would follow.

As I survey the landscape, my heart exudes with sorrow for all those I see of abandoned faith who have neglected, renounced or either forgot the sacrifices of those who made a way for their future. Selfish lives, selfish choices; forgotten dreams; reinventing themselves by disarming their past.

The only material possession I have of my Father is a watch I kept as a reminder of the bonds of love we shared.

One month after his death and on the same day of the month, it stopped ticking. As I looked at the face of the watch, the time indicated *"5 seconds to midnight"!* The hour and minute hands on the dial pointed to True North at 12:00, but before transitioning into a new day, there were 5 seconds remaining.

I pondered on that thought for quite some time. It spoke volumes to me; *"It's not over until it's over".* Regardless of the appearance of things, we may think there is no time left to reclaim. Whatever we purpose to do in life; do it while it is yet day for night will soon follow. There is still time remaining to maximize on our dreams that may have eluded us because of our misfortunes.

I Saw the Light

For years, I stood on the peripheral of God's Kingdom, watching from the outside with curiosity. The lessons of Vietnam would not allow the discovery of truth other than the truth of my suffering. There were many nights camped out in the jungle I wanted so desperately to go home. Often I lay gazing into the heavens crying from within with a quivering voice of surrender; *"If there is a God up there, deliver me out of my misery".* As usual, no one answered; the heavens gave no indication that my voice ever penetrated the barriers of the restricted atmosphere of the noise of cannons firing through the air, machine guns, mortars, gunships and the fear occupying my heart.

As a soldier in Vietnam locked in a battle of survival, I was an unwilling child launched into turmoil with fear as my only company. I searched for light to bring healing to my soul in the midst of hostilities, death and the daily confrontation of overwhelming trepidation. I was surrounded by God's grace which should have been sufficient, but I was blinded by my fears; failing to discover His Presence protecting me. I wandered endlessly looking for something to attach my hope to but still could not see the "*Hope of Ages*" that was sustaining me. I was defeated; trapped inside of a conscience that would not release me.

I took note of the lives of those who had forsaken all and denied the natural world access for an *"invisible force"* that was beyond my recognition. I noticed they were being guided down an indistinguishable path paralleling my steps and speaking uncommon words from another dimension of existence. As I continued to drown in a sea of misery stirred with emotions of fear, I often heard the words echoing from the Brothers of Faith; *"Keep the Faith my Brother"*.

I followed them from a distance and observed the performance of powers that witnessed to me delivering hope where there was no hope. It became a provocation, challenging the foundation of all that I believed. I discovered that there was a deeper power with the ability to see things in the dark more than I could recognize in the light.

Upon my return home from the warzone, I fell on my knees and prayed a prayer of thanksgiving. I was grateful that I was alive seemingly bearing no physical scars of pain; but the weeping persisted. I was lost with nowhere to go and no one to talk to. Day after day with no peace to be found; I wandered from one extreme to the other. I was in a search to find myself but I didn't know how.

While searching through the entanglements that had such a grip on my spirit, a soft spoken word of hope connected to my anguish. It was the voice of my Mother; the voice of love that never abandoned me. She said, *"Son, come home"*.

The disappointments of my Father in my quandary loomed in my memory. As I struggled to get free from the connected web of confusion that had me bound, the words of my Father's song began singing in my ear; *"There is a bright side somewhere, don't you rest until you find it, there is a bright side somewhere"*. The song continued resonating within and would not stop; *"I will go into my secret closet and I will fall down on my knees"*. With a weeping spirit, I found the passion for tears. It humbled me and again I bowed on bended knees.

Suddenly, the healing power of my tears flooded the chambers of my heart. The condemnation lifted from my conscience. I was being made whole again. I was ushered into that place of surrender; no more heartache; no more pain and suffering; no more frustration and confusion; no more weeping. The taste of freedom finally arrived.

The power to weep had left me; buried in the sea of forgetfulness. I was free! Free from conviction of my failures; free to reclaim life and believe again. On bended knee, I cried with a loud voice, *"Lord, open my eyes that I may see; open my ears that I may hear, loose my tongue that I may speak"*. Suddenly, I could hear with clarity and my eyes opened to truth. I began to hear voices from afar calling me.

As I looked up, I saw that the heavens were opened. Then a thundering Voice from above spoke and the Earth began to shake. The tombstone of defeat planted on my destiny was shattered into pieces and with a shout, the Voice from above said *"loose him"*. The shackles of my heart, mind, body and soul released me from a valley littered in despair into the flourishing pastures of the newness of life.

The gravitational powers that held me earthbound with such gripping constraints on my destiny responded in kind and released their hold on me. I was drawn upward, accelerating into a higher dimension; *"learning to fly again"*. Not bound by the captivity of the world any longer, I began to soar in the Presence of The Almighty far above any heights I had ever attained. The Wind of His Spirit embraced me and thrust me even higher. I crossed the barriers of time and seasons finally arriving in a world full of love and peace.

With gates of pearls and floors mirrored in gold, I entered the pearly gates celebrating in a dance I had never known. With arms flailing and my body twisting, the strings of my heart began to play as the Angels joined in a symphony of praise. Heaven's Choir began to sing *"Sweet Lamb of God"* at the sight of His Rod.

I saw my Mother shouting with joy with a crown on her head that was minus one star. The peculiarity of her crown caused me to ponder. Deep within, with my soul overwhelmed, I knew then I was the vacant star missing from her crown. In the blink of an eye, His Spirit escorted me to a chair where I was seated beside a Chair of gold; the Chair called Righteousness. A Scroll was handed to me; I opened it and read the word; *"HOPE"*.

I had encountered the *"Hope of Ages"*. I could not see His Face but I felt His Presence. I became weak from the power of

His love that stretched endlessly throughout all eternity. I was bathed in the power of His expectation and adorned with Wings of His Spirit and realized; *"Now, I Can Truly Fly"*.

With the voice of His Spirit blasting in my ear as a sound of a trumpet giving summons of His Power, the vision of my future was sealed in the Scroll of *"HOPE"*. In a trilogy of sound as a united symphony, He echoed His command, *"Return to the Mountain"*.

Armed with the sealed Scroll of sheepskin written in the *"Blood of the Lamb"* clutch in my hand; I traveled through the heavens with majestic speed as a comet of fire and returned with the Scroll dripping with Blood cleansing the Earth from wickedness and sin. I landed on top of a Mountain; Elijah was waiting, doubled in His mantle. With an urgency, he cast His mantle upon me and said; *"Not by My Might, nor by My Power, but by My Spirit said the Lord"*.

Just as quickly as he appeared; he disappeared. It was now time to descend the Mountain. With the Scroll of *"HOPE"*, I now began to walk; step by step into the preparation of His Grace that was waiting my obedience. Every step is a step of faith into a divine encounter only discovered by the depth of His gifting. Wherever I go, the Scroll is opened and ready to read:

> *"Do not ask the Lord to guide your footsteps, if you are not willing to move your feet!"*
> (Rodney Fritzgerald)

When the scroll of life is finished, I will adorn my wings again and take flight. Not to the top of the Mountain but from *"whence I came, searching for the crown with a vacant star"*. I will take my place in my Mother's crown as a sparkling jewel and we will rejoice together in His Eternal Light. As I prepare for the stars of my own crown to be adorned with precious stones from generations that will follow; Heaven is waiting for me and I cherish the hope someday I will hear the trumpets blow. From a life of despair to arisen height of the Mountain, the message of the Scroll gives hope to the weary;

"Faint not in well doing. For soon shall be your reward"

Chapter 12

I have been to an extraordinary number of funerals over the past two years. It's a reminder to make the best of my days and not squander the good that I can do while I yet have the strength to do it. Seemingly, at every funeral I have attended, there is a special anthem sung written nearly three centuries ago that still reverberates with the same authentic passion that humbled a forsaken heart in the calamitous straits of the "Middle Passage". I often wonder when I hear the melody being sung by synchronizing voices caught up in the passion of such a compelling story, at times even moved to tears;

> *"Is there recognition of the legacy of the author's intentions"?*

There is a compelling testimony that is left in the archives of our times; so enriched in hope sprouting the power of faith that has manifested in the lives of multitudes who were lost in the darkened seas of unbelief. It is the testimony of John Newton. His testimony still has power that speaks beyond the grave as a legacy of a redemptive life saved by the delivering power of God's grace.

It was grace encountered that altered his path at the beckoning of his cry in travailing seas. When the anguish of life descended upon him in hopeless despair, he cried for the only hope he knew who had *"Power"* to calm the seas and rescue his soul from the shores of death. His journey began as a self-proclaimed wretch undone but ended by seeing the *"Light"* piercing through a raging storm. The same storm which raised havoc upon the seas ushered in deliverance so mighty and great.

"With a repentant heart and no place to hide, he surrendered in humility, broken in his pride."

Amazing grace! (how sweet the sound)
That sav'd a wretch like me!
I once was lost, but now am found,
Was blind, but now I see.

'Twas grace that taught my heart to fear,
And grace my fears reliev'd;
How precious did that grace appear,
The hour I first believ'd!

Thro' many dangers, toils and snares,
I have already come;
'Tis grace has brought me safe thus far,
And grace will lead me home.

The Lord has promis'd good to me,
His word my hope secures;
He will my shield and portion be,
As long as life endures.

Yes, when this flesh and heart shall fail,
And mortal life shall cease;
I shall possess, within the veil,
A life of joy and peace.

The earth shall soon dissolve like snow,
The sun forbear to shine;
But God, who call'd me here below,
Will be forever mine.

Who could have written such compelling words with such sustaining power that has been secured throughout the ages? What power prevailed in the troubling seas that offered deliverance so mighty and great transforming an unbelieving heart into an ambassador of faith? The author of those words was a self-proclaimed wretch who once was lost but then was found, saved by God's Amazing Grace.

John Newton was born in London July 24, 1725; the son of a merchant ship commander who sailed the Mediterranean. When John was eleven, he went to sea with his Father and made six voyages with him before the elder Newton retired. A father's love and care has an empowering influence purposed to shape character and integrity into the lives of his generation. It is often what is seeded in his heart are seeds born of their kind that begin to take root in the developing lives of his children. Like a father, a son blossoms into his likeness spreading his own seeds to fulfill the cycle of life.

In 1744, John was impressed into service following the footprints already waiting for his discovery. He was commissioned to serve on a man-of-war, the H. M. S. Harwich. When he found conditions on board intolerable, he deserted but was soon captured, publicly flogged and demoted from midshipman to common seaman. Finally at his own request, he was exchanged into service on a *"Slave Ship"*, which took him to the coast of Sierra Leone, Africa.

John then became the servant of a slave trader and was brutally abused. It should be noted that if our choices lead us to serving men, by default we will inherit their abuses and decisions that can make our lives miserable. Our destiny has already been predetermined from our beginnings. To alter that path is a subjection to chance; a chance that can lead to a random search subtracting years from our lives.

Early in 1748, Newton was rescued by a sea captain who had known his father. He ultimately became captain of his own ship, a ship that would determine his fate in an undiscovered path waiting in the channels of faith. Life is a journey even though our endings will forever be entombed in our beginnings. The Apostle Paul started out persecuting Christians but the result of the predetermined end of his destiny proved he would become one of the greatest revelators of our time.

Newton became the captain of a *"Ship of Captives"*; those enslaved in such horrific captivity, the weak and feeble whose choices were stripped from the domain of human dignity and respect. He became a slave trader pursuing the path of his predecessor, capitalizing on the sufferings, fears and tears of those without a voice to defend. The entombed cries of mercy fell upon deafen ears as the human cargo was chained in bellows away from his sight. He crossed the *"Middle Passage"* with no conscience of remorse, but little did he know; he would have a passage of his own.

Although Newton had some early religious instruction from his mother, who had died when he was a child, he had long since given up any religious convictions. Sometimes in life, separation from the passion of love centered in our hearts can cause an interruption of our beliefs. Our emotions will give cause to our wavering, dislodging any hope to continue in the path set before us. It is so easy to lose focus reaching in the darkness of a separated past that does not lend its power to determine what lies ahead.

As destiny would prevail, on an unsuspecting voyage, Newton struggled to steer the ship through a violent storm. He experienced what he referred to as his *"Great Deliverance."* Judgment always comes even when we may have thought we have escaped God's searching eyes. He recorded in his journal; *"When all seemed lost and the ship would surely sink"*; he did what any of us would do when facing imminent danger. He cried out from the bellows of despair with the hope of deliverance, *"Lord, have mercy upon Us."* He was as the thief veiled on the cross next to Jesus on Golgotha's Hill, crying for mercy with his destiny lurking in the shadows of death.

Newton's cry for help was not only for himself, but for all those who were *"committed into his trust"*. Was his motivation to protect the cargo of suffering souls as to not lose his profit? Or was it the genuineness of his heart reflective of a revolution going on in his conscience? Both paths would result in the same conclusion; he would change with a higher priority bearing a conscience of conviction. An unselfish heart bearing the burdens of trust is a fellowship that will unite the power of God to our faith and move the hand of His Spirit when the sincerity of our plea meets His Ear. Often times in our distress, we inadvertently call upon the Lord's name seeking help beyond our weaknesses.

As a wretched undone crying for help in the wilderness of despair, he searched for an answer when there was no one to hear. With waves raging in the angry seas and the relentless winds threatening to the point of death, God's grace and mercy stilled the storm. Without an anchor in faith to attract the Ear of God in the midst of troubling seas, the desperate cry of the humbled will yield His Grace, proving the greatness of a power we routinely reject.

Within the Veil

We were ushered into this life with a cry and shall surely return the life that was given. In the waning moments of life's betrayal, we all will cry from abandoned love; *"My Lord, My Lord why have You forsaken me"*. It is the cry for the embracing power of love that is separating from us; *"Lord receive my Spirit, wrap me in Your bosom, comfort me in the solace of Your Love"*. It is a lonely hour of solitude in an eternal search to rest in peace.

> *Yes, when this flesh and heart shall fail,*
> *And mortal life shall cease;*
> *I shall possess, within the veil,*
> *A life of joy and peace.*
> *The earth shall soon dissolve like snow,*
> *The sun forbear to shine;*
> *But God, who call'd me here below,*
> *Will be forever mine.*

Later in his cabin, Newton reflected on what he had said and began to believe that God had answered him through the storm and that grace had begun to work for him. For the rest of his life he observed the anniversary of May 10, 1748 as the day of his *"Conversion"*, a day of humiliation in which he subjected his will to the *"Supreme Authority of all creation"*. His journey in search of truth took twenty-three years before he discovered the Light.

> *"Thro' many dangers, toils and snares, I have already come; 'tis grace has bro't me safe thus far, and grace will lead me home."*

There is light waiting to be discovered in the center of all our circumstances; waiting to embrace our humility for the greater consequences that is laid in the path before us.

Newton continued in the slave trade for a time after his conversion; however, he saw to it that the slaves under his care were treated humanely. Deliverance is a process not always so immediate to recover truth in its fullness. It is as Lazarus who received resurrection but had to be delivered from the connections to his past. His hands and feet had to be freed from bondage that held him captive. His mind had to be renewed with the daily washing of the Word to prove *"What is the Good, Acceptable and Perfect Will of God"*.

The discovery of Newton's destiny was revealed amidst the raging storm in a broken vessel of hope. But within his soul, the quiet storm of *"God's Eternal Fire"* was ignited, brewing an aroma of humility to restore unto others their dignity and pride. He made the decision to follow The Almighty and became an ambassador of faith. He ultimately became a voice exposing the cruelty and inhumane nature of slavery; an abolitionist he would become, a proponent of freedom to all mankind. Once a man is free, principally it should become his desire to see all men free.

Capitalism and Greed

John Newton's original motivation of exporting slaves was born out of greed even to the point of sacrificing the life of another human being. The greed of capitalism is very infectious. Generations have come and gone and the strength of their years has been passed on through legacies of adoptive greed; which is to simply say inheritance.

The love of money has corrupted the hearts and minds of an endless generation of people. The principles of capitalism are rooted right here in our own back yard. To some of us it is as close as a stroke of a key on our keyboard as we surf with vigilance to protect our investments and profits even though they may have come as a profit from the blood diamonds of Liberia, mercury from the gold of Ghana or from chemicals such as Agent Orange and other toxins existing within our own borders.

When the stock market crumbled, some lost their entire savings while the capitalist recovered with the buffer of tax payer's dollars to exceed their bottom line in monumental proportions. Today the Stock Market is recording record highs due to speculations and manipulation setting the stage for a return to chaos that visited this country. Have they not learnt lessons from our past: *"don't return to your own vomit"*?

The success of those at the top comes at a cost to those at the bottom. The principle of capitalism can't be validated without a victim. It was born on the backs of those who endured horrific suffering during the slave trade. The cheapest labor that was available was forced labor; not hard work that came from using one's own God given strength and talents but manipulating those weakened and dependent satisfying the thirst of the greedy and influential. Capitalism essentially means capitalizing on someone's grief and misfortune as to insure the maximum profitability from their sufferings. Don't believe me; try losing your job and miss a payment. It don't matter; credit card, mortgage, car payment and we will see whether your interest rate remain the same with fees and penalties to match.

The Wall Street we know today has been transformed as a center of commerce with ascetic appeal leading all the way up to its doorsteps. At this country's beginning, Wall Street was an open market where slaves just arriving across the Atlantic were sold; lined up in shackles *"up against a wall"*, and sold to the highest bidder. It's very ironic that Africans *(Black Gold)* built the wall and were sold on the wall sealing their fate for the struggles they would face.

> *The very name "Wall Street" is born of slavery, with enslaved Africans building a wall in 1653 to protect Dutch settlers from Indian raids. In 1711 the city's Common Council established a Meal Market at Wall and Water streets for hiring slave labor and auctioning enslaved Africans who disembarked in Manhattan after their arduous transatlantic journey. (13)*

Perhaps, it is a given truth that slavery has gone on since the beginning of time; the dominance of one culture over a lesser empowered civilization. It is very painful to see that this type of behavior is still going on in the 21st century.

Generationally, there is no denying that the consequence of slave market trading continues to loom deeply in the psyche of Black families in very subtle and subconscious ways. Reminders are still there because of bigotry and racism which as a Nation we refuse to address. The Black family structure was destroyed during the slave market trade; separation of mothers from fathers; sisters from brothers; children from parents and for most, never to see each other again. With no other means of survival, everyone had to endure the devastation of a life of servitude.

The stigmas of Black family life are still being played out as talking points of the *"denialist"*, our modern day oppressors. I still remain unconvinced of the Founders intention of *"one Law that applies to all equal in distribution"*. During the time when framing the Constitution, many of the signers were hypocritically ambitious with very ambiguous practices described by the standard of their own language.

In today's culture, declining family structure is not just a unique phenomenon within the Black community but now, seemingly it is more of the norm amongst our general population for an array of reasons. I believe the greater influence being *"we have lost our spiritual and moral compass"* by pursing the vanities of life; artificially replacing materiality for spirituality. We have given power to the beast to reign as an altered perception of our human existence.

Everyone likes nice and elaborate things and so do I. But to sacrifice one's integrity for the acquisition of temporary pleasures remains of paramount concern with me. Greed is a very destructive force that is no different from pride. Both are exaggerations fueled by fear as a threat to one's preeminence.

Far too many Black men, as of today, remain in shackles; some elective by the choices they made; some because of the imposition of societal norms and some are systemic due to our cultural legacy. The way our penal system is structured, it disproportionately incarcerates Black men because of the color of their skin. How I have often heard the articulation; *"there is balance in the scales of justice"* as to not consider the causes for the inequities that have been systemic throughout our history. I believe that education, poverty, jobs and quality medical care are instigators more so than morality which parallels across the spectrum amongst all cultures.

Recently, I went to a local hardware store to purchase an air filter. The cashier who rung up my purchase noticed I was wearing a black baseball cap with the inscription New York embroidered on the front. I guess in small talk he politely asked me had I ever been to New York. I looked at him as if to say; *"Why are you asking me such a stupid question"*. He was a kid maybe no more than in his early twenties. I facetiously answered; *"No"*. He then suggested that I should visit sometime not realizing that I had already *"been there, done that"*. He was very proud to have been from New York and alluded to the fact that New York was the *"epic center of the world"*. In my response, I said; *"you need to come out of the weeds"*.

While driving home, I pondered rather intently on his words (*epic center of the world*). It triggered a response in my emotions as I began to rebuff the exclusion that there wasn't anything as monumental as the City of Stone. My mind immediately focused on all of our National Monuments but most importantly our National Veteran Commemorations. I concluded that the *"epic center of the world"* can be found in 3.9 million graves of our soldiers who sacrificed their lives. Without them, none of the world's democracies would exist.

Homeless in America

Conceivably, one could rest their laurels based on the fact that New York is one of the world's largest cities, the center of finance, fashion, entertainment and enormous wealth. But despite the wealth, there is poverty and homelessness of abysmal proportions. To be homeless in America is a tragedy beyond excuse. Because of *"American Exceptionalism"*, we have emerged to be the leader in the free world but yet we do not put much value in securing the lives of many that are without, particularly our veterans. The long arm of compassion extends abroad with aid and influence flowing in the billions but we have not prioritized in taking care of our own. Have we truly embraced the price for freedom?

Demographics of Homeless Veterans
12% of the homeless adult population are veterans
20% of the male homeless population are veterans
68% reside in principal cities
32% reside in suburban/rural areas
51% of individual homeless veterans have disabilities
50% have serious mental illness
70% have substance abuse problems
51% are white males, compared to 38% of non-veterans
50% are age 51 or older, compared to 19% non-veterans

America's homeless veterans have served in World War II, the Korean War, Cold War, Vietnam War, Grenada, Panama, Lebanon, Persian Gulf War, Afghanistan and Iraq (OEF/OIF), and the military's anti-drug cultivation efforts in South America. *Nearly half of homeless veterans served during the Vietnam era.* Two-thirds served our country for at least three years, and one-third were stationed in a war zone. About 1.4 million other veterans, meanwhile, are considered at risk of homelessness due to poverty, lack of support networks, and dismal living conditions in overcrowded or substandard housing. (8)

Regardless of all our negatives, there still is a positive. We still have time to rectify our wrongs if we choose to remain under allegiance to our declarations;

"One Nation, Under God, Indivisible with Liberty and Justice for All."

"Eternity is born in each and every one of us. A man who says he believes in nothing is a man who has no place left for the sun to shine."

Chapter 13

How many were killed on their first and last day in country?

There were 997 killed on their arrival day.
There were 1443 killed on their departure day. (11)

Years ago, I bought a parakeet from a local pet store. She was a beautiful bird with spotted feathers of green and blue. I contemplated a name for her and after much pondering; I called her *"Rhema"*, which means the *"Living Word"*. I would sit for hours adoring her beauty but somehow, I felt the pain of her loneliness. You see, her home was a cage encompassed in iron. As a consequence, I would always leave her door opened with the freedom to fly.

From one room to the next, she would spread her wings and perch upon the window's ledge with nowhere else to go. She still was a caged bird deprived of her elements. Back and forth she flew from the iron cage to the cage of windows with invisible panes. I discerned her desire to be free as she often peered through the glass pane of her captivity searching into the sky for familiar tweets of a sound of her kind. To satisfy my conscience of the indictment of her loneliness, I decided in her best interest to buy another bird; after all two are better than one. Loneliness is familiar to us all; always searching for protection that only two can provide.

> *Two are better than one, Because they have a good reward for their labor. For if they fall, one will lift up his companion. But woe to him who is alone when he falls, For he has no one to help him up. Again, if two lie down together, they will keep warm; But how can one be warm alone? Though one may be overpowered by another, two can withstand him. And a threefold cord is not quickly broken.*

I thoughtfully considered a pairing name for my new friend. I decided to name him *"Logos"* which literally means the *"Written Word"*. Logos also was a beautiful bird arrayed with brilliant colors. To my surprise, Rhema and Logos bonded instantly, chirping together beak to beak serenading in a harmony of mellow tweets. They were like two eagles locking talons swan dancing high in the atmosphere.

They flew together room to room following the same beaten path still searching for freedom. I discovered birds of a feather do flock together. When their bonds were strengthened, they strayed away from my touch, with no further need of me to fill the void. I was comforted to know that they had each other, but still the pejorative lingering of my conscience weighed heavily upon my spirit causing me to consider that now I had two birds trapped conspiring to be free.

Their bond of fellowship was strengthened as having a communion of bread and wine being shared over a friendship of memories. With their beating hearts joined together as a compass of love, the synergy of their togetherness was itself an expression of freedom; an expression of two hearts beating as one that never stops beating, still wanting to be free.

Lessons from Africa

On my first journey to Africa nearly twenty years in my not so distant past, I discovered a truth through introspection that changed my perspective of myself and my views of the history that produced me. I had engaged in a conversation with a young African man named Ramos who raised a question that challenged the consistency of my fabric. He said;

> *"Despite how impoverished I am without the comforts and material amenities of life and the prosperity you are enjoying in America, I have something you don't."*

As I contemplated his thoughts, I searched to consider the possibilities of his words. In my immediate assessment, I determined that I had money, house, education, family, faith and the enjoyment of the pleasures of life. I could go where I wanted, do what I wanted, when I wanted and get what I wanted! It was in dire contrast to the meagerness of his conditions. What could have possibly been missing? He said to me very simply; *"I am free"*.

He extrapolated his thoughts that began to connect with my feelings that were masked in denial. He explained to me that his generations were never shackled in chains, stripped of their human identity, disgraced and hated to the end of such a cruel system of Chattel Slavery that was imposed on my ancestors. Even with Apartheid and the wickedness of its framers fell short of the *"Dark Knights of destruction wearing sheets of white"* while burning in the night. Those who thirsted for freedom faced the challenge of intimidating fear and rejection by the hands of an enemy resolved beyond compromise. The Dark Knights haven't ceased their campaign of terror; still adopting new stealthy methods in their failing attempts to further suppress any advances of a generation determined in their commitment for justice and freedom.

Ramos generations never had to endure the legacy of struggles inflicted upon my Elders who were ever so wounded in their cries of despair. The cruelty of murder, rape, beatings, lynching and the dehumanizing classification of not being fully human is a testament never to be forgotten. Terror is terror whether it is in the Middle East or here in our own backyard. A legacy of centuries of hatred and bigotry is not so easy to overcome.

American culture is rooted in violence; from its violent beginnings to the sophistication of ideas and practices that still limits the true power of expression of all its citizenry in ascertaining justice. Ramos discerned that I was still bound generationally to the place of sufferings and persecutions that was passed on through the linage of time. What I was still fighting for, he already possessed; *"The right to be"*.

I know the feelings of the caged bird. Unshackled from fetters of iron and a door open to a path of restricted freedom, I continue to peer into the sky from windows sealed by glass, longing to surface on the other side. The struggles of my ancestry are woven into my fabric with tearing displays of an unsettled pursuit of justice bearing the burdens of poverty, inequity and rejection because of the color of my skin. I am brown chocolate and not the whiter shade of pale.

Emotional trauma born from the consequences of bigotry, hatred and the enslaving of one's mind is a horror that has no justifying end. The common respect for all of God's creation is a standard for the civil minded to render the rightful justice to all of humanity.

I took note of Ramos assessment even though I knew he had a different battle of his own; the battle of occupying powers of murderers and thieves exploiting his land and restricting the flow of his sovereignty; but he gave me reason to consider. He had struck a vein that flowed as the crucified blood of Jesus from a cross that fell upon the grounds of rejection. Rejection is a systemic truth that inhibits freedom of our gifts to flourish in the fertile soils of life.

The power of ancestral spirits has a prevailing affect in the subconscious mind of our generation. Whether we accept this as truth, there can be no denial of its power over the collective conscience of our existence. Our struggles remain even until today, fighting for justice and equality in a cold and senseless world void of the seeds of compassion. The liberating power of God's love is the only liberating power that can free the heart. Love covers a multitude of sin and lays a path to peace and the healing powers of forgiveness.

"Eternity is born in each and every one of us. A man who says he believes in nothing is man who has no place left for the sun to shine"

Night Waters

As I peer into the night, I see the silhouette of two lonely hearts searching in the dark. I can't see their faces, just images of those navigating the passion of night. Masked in insecurity and desire to be made whole in the dark of passion; the betrayal of darkness leads them only to chance. Darkness is a chance; the chance of uncertainties masquerading as truth.

In the retreat of darkness without a compass of guidance of the light of day, the light of the moon and stars give way to reappearing shadows celebrating intimate treasures of the seclusion of night. With beating hearts yearning for breath in the heat of evening, the friendliness of darkness embrace in passion as a never ending journey wavering in the night waters of chance.

As the moon of darkness eclipses the light of the sun, they clutch in hope, bonding together for an experience that only darkness brings. While waiting for the dawn of day in search of light to see their way, they drift with the listing tide riding the waves of chance. The uncertainty of chance has captured another vessel hiding in the shadows with no reflective light.

Two ships sailing in the dark are two ships that have missed the calling of light headed for chance encounters that only darkness brings.

Chapter 14

Door of No Return
Forgotten Dreams

Edward S. Krukowski, Charles P. Sparks, Ernest J. Halvorson, Robert G. Armstrong, Theodore B. Phillips, Eugene Richardson and Valmore W. Bourque were serving together and all seven were killed together on October 24, 1964, in Cambodia. They are located on panel 1E, lines 067 - 069. Cambodia had a total of 520 veterans that were killed or missing in action. (12)

I wasn't prepared for the emotional roller coaster ride I experienced on my first and only visit to the historic *"Vietnam Memorial Wall"*. It is a memory that will forever be seared in my conscience. For years since its dedication in 1982, I have driven by those black stones hundreds of times but never had the impulse to stop. I was very reluctant to the idea of traveling that far back in time to embrace memories that were remarkably fresh in my mind. Whether it was neighborhood friends who perished on the battlefield or Brothers I served with in the jungles of Southeast Asia who lost their lives to such a dreadful ending; I never mastered the courage to encounter my fears at the *"Wall of the Dead"*.

I discovered my tears were my greatest fear. For so many years I held back weeping denying the presence of pain that had existed up until then 43 years. Recently, I participated in a trip to the *"Wall"* to honor the lives of those who made the ultimate contribution of war; their blood. *"Life is in the Blood"* but after blood yields its final contribution, there is nothing left but memories of a forsaken past.

It was an eerie sense of awakening to look at the endless rows of black granite stones engraved with the names of 58,000 souls offered as incense in the nostrils of those who perverted their sacrifices. Even though their bodies returned home, their blood was distributed as fertilizer on the grounds of a foreign land. The blood of the fallen is sacred and stands as a witness against man's insensibilities and malice motives.

A Cadence to Remember

The jungles of Vietnam have muffled the voices of those still crying for justice but I can still hear them. I will always remember them; respect them and cherish their legacy. I want so desperately to turn back the hands of time to redeem them with the same nurturing love as a father nurtures his child to hold them; to comfort them; to teach them; to show them a better world than all who were against them; who despised them; who ridiculed them; who used them and forgot them. I would nurture their wounds with the healing balm of compassion to restore them; walk with them; laugh with them and enjoy the pleasures of life with them. Like a Weeping Willow, I continue to cry for them because I believe in them; I'll fight for them and do everything no one else will do for them. Until our lives reunite and no more tears left to shed, I, the dreamer will dream for them; dreams of an everlasting peace; a peace that exist beyond the boundaries of greed, pride, malice, rejection and self-righteousness.

INDEPENDENCE DAY
"RED, WHITE AND BLUE"

Red....... the blood we shed; White.......the innocence we lost;
Blue.........abated justice;
Stripes.......open wounds salted in suffering and pain;
Stars....... teardrops which continues to flow.
Why praise the Wall of the Dead and not the Living.
The Dead can't talk but yet They weep; They can't see but
yet They hear; They can't feel but yet They moan.
Silenced........... forever!
Erase our wounds? They are still there! Conscience bleeding?
Quite intriguing;
Some survived made it out alive; We are not going anywhere!
...............The audacity to Live?................

"Brother Gate"

The human costs of the long conflict were harsh for all involved. Not until 1995 did Vietnam release its official estimate of war dead: as many as 2 million civilians on both sides and some 1.1 million North Vietnamese and Viet Cong fighters. The U.S. military has estimated that between 200,000 and 250,000 South Vietnamese soldiers died in the war. In 1982 the Vietnam Veterans Memorial was dedicated in Washington, D.C., inscribed with the names of 57,939 members of U.S. armed forces who had died or were missing as a result of the war. Over the following years, additions to the list have brought the total past 58,200. (At least 100 names on the memorial are those of servicemen who were actually Canadian citizens.) Among other countries that fought for South Vietnam on a smaller scale, South Korea suffered more than 4,000 dead, Thailand about 350, Australia more than 500, and New Zealand some three dozen.

www.britannica.com/events/Vietnam-War

In God We Trust

58,000 Souls
319,000 Quarts of Blood
In God....................We Trust
..
Half a century later.......We're waiting!
Time is ticking…...............We're still waiting!
Tick Tock……………......…..…………………..!
Blue Line Flat Line..It's too late!
...................."No More Blood Left To Give"....................

"Brother Gate"

There are 22 countries represented on the Memorial. (8)

Upon my first visit to Cape Coast Castle located in Cape Coast, Ghana, the ancestral departure for so many of our African American descendants, I did not have any idea what I was to experience. Just as the Vietnam Memorial, Cape Coast Castle echoed the sentiment of injustice and crimes against life. Even though geographically they are worlds apart, they both share as victims of the same imperialistic influence rooted in America's divisive history. The motivations may be different for the sacrifice of so many lives, however the end result is still the same; more sacrificial blood corrupted on the land and in the seas.

Cape Coast Castle is a commercial fort sitting on the Gold Coast of West Africa as a gateway to the Atlantic Ocean. It was originally built by the Europeans for trade in timber and gold but was later used in the Trans-Atlantic slave trade to hold slaves before they were loaded onto ships and sold in the Americas and Caribbean Islands. As a beacon still standing approaching 400 years, it bears testimony of the atrocities of slavery.

Ghana was a conquered land because of its wealth of natural resources particularly gold, but more significantly, it became a major exporter of human commodities in fettered chains. The slave trade was prolific and competitive. Spread out across Africa's West Coast, nearly 30 Slave Castles were erected as transfer centers transporting slaves across the *"Middle Passage"* that bridged West Africa to the Americas and Caribbean shores. Between the 16th and 19th century, a human highway across the Atlantic continued until 1865.

As I toured the grounds hearing the horrific recall of the *"Testimonies of Sufferings"*, I asked my guide a question and waited for an answer I was not ready to hear. I asked him; *"How many were lost at sea?"* He gave a very riveting reply. He said there was no definitive answer but gave the most accurate assessment based on records: *"Forty Million!"* The number of slaves who died at sea was so great that sharks learned to follow the slave routes because they fed on the bodies thrown overboard. Everyone in the crowd wept! An eerie silence had dampened all of our expectations; turning our weeping into mourning. Just as the wailings of Jesus in the Garden of Gethsemane, my spirit wailed for the forty million dreams buried beneath the sea. The *"Middle Passage"* became a graveyard of souls as stepping stones for generations that would follow. Just the thought alone of what it took to survive such a treacherous journey and weather the storms of centuries of persecution is a testament within itself.

Needless to say, this was a holocaust by its own right. We never hear of those sacrificial offerings as a cost for our freedom; always pointing the finger of distraction away from ownership of our own failings. It is easy to recognize fault in others, but the blinding nature of pride binds to ignorance and is visibly troubling and offensive in its portrayal of denial. At times truth can be very punishing when we are not fully prepared to accept its revelation which could inadvertently shatter all that we believed. It has the propensity of influencing our decisions in very dramatic ways.

We all had come to the Castle seeking a connection to the place of our beginnings before our ancestors were carted off to a land thousands of miles in the distant winds of unfamiliarity but we encountered more than we expected. As we continued the tour from dungeon to dungeon, the heaviness in my heart was unbearable. How inhumane can a human being discount the value of human life and suffering of another. Left on the floors and walls were the imprints of those who gouged their fingers into the concrete in agony; wailing collectively with voices that traveled the seas. I guess I am one of the lucky ones; my ancestors survived a horrific journey for my freedom. I value it dearly and very grateful for their sacrifice; truly I will never forget.

Eventually, we came to a gate that opened to the sea. It was named the *"Door of No Return"*. The clanging of iron and the shrilling tears of indescribable agony of broken spirits, they made the voyage in the *"Middle of the Passage"*. Shackled and sold as cattle on the open market, the uncompassionate cruelty of a new master emerged violating the human principle of respect and dignity for the sake of filthy lucre.

Capitalism replaced compassion; greed and self-righteous pride became a substitute for suffering and pain. I render no condemnation to my oppressors; *"Envy not thine oppressor and choose none of his ways. For vengeance is mine saith the Lord".* For the rewards of my sufferings, I render the healing power love born from an unconditional stream of forgiveness.

The seas never get full of their tears neither does those salty drippings cease to wash away anguish from our countenance. At times it will cry out in a raging storm like hurricane forces screaming in the night. From east to west across the Atlantic, the path of the hurricane is a continual reminder retracing the route of sufferings. It is the vengeance of souls riding the winds of judgment as a reminder of centuries of injustice that is still seeded in the heart of our Nation.

In North America, the landscape was purified of its indigenous occupants, the North American Indians. We forget we are living as occupiers in a conquered land. While Native Americans primarily remain segregated on reservations, they maintain their identity as a separate Nation. The price they paid for the genocidal annihilation of their people and culture can't justify the *"Treaties of Blood".*

The *"Door of No Return"* has been transformed into a beacon of hope searching the seas to reclaim what was lost. It has been renamed the *"Door of Return"* calling back to its shores those separated by the middle divide of a raging tempest that will never be forgotten. It is without a doubt *"Amazing Grace"* has sustained our generation throughout the ages as a testimony of survival in our continual pursuit for justice. Hatred is not the answer, only the transparency of love, peace and forgiveness will restore the caged bird his flight into the open window of heaven.

The Middle Passage

From east to west I came riding the waves at the eclipse of day.
I was the Voice draped in despair in a wilderness of tears
separated from my land; not even a glimpse of comfort being
tossed by waves of an angry sea, I made the voyage in the
"Middle of the Passage"
across an endless ocean with depths unknown
"The Spirit of Currents" protecting a valley of bones.
With the moon glowing in the eve of day, I say a prayer for the
fallen souls riding the currents below;
Cherishing their memories, I take my bow, flooded with tears to
quiet the storm.
Passion, compassion has drifted into the hot tempered winds of
retreat; leaving only the distant fumes of a land that smelled so
sweet.
Spices, nectar with an aroma burning with the gift of fire,
glimmering in a blaze of embers borrowed from the light.
With the fire of night burning so bright, bellowing vapors of
memories as a guide in the light.
How sweet the sound of ancient past, the sound of drums calling
me in the night.
Silent wind, silent Voices speaking so loud, calling me home in
this sea of clouds; Where seas end is where they begin, show me
the way to that distant wind. Radiant glow of this hope unknown,
take me back where I've always been.

References

(1) www.ask.com/wiki/Charles_McMahon_and_Darwin_Judge?lang=en
(2) www.ask.com/wiki/Charles_McMahon_and_Darwin_Judge?lang=en
(3) www.touchthewall.org/facts.html#1v
(4) www.touchthewall.org/facts.html#1v
(5) www.ask.com/wiki/Charles_McMahon_and_Darwin_Judge?lang=en
(6) www.touchthewall.org/facts.html#1v
(7) www. touchthewall.org/facts.html#1v
(8) http://ichv.org/index.php/news/media/background &statistics/#incarcerated
(9) www.touchthewall.org/facts.html#1v
(10) www.touchthewall.org/facts.html#1v
(11) www.touchthewall.org/facts.html#1v
(12) www.touchthewall.org/facts.html#1v
(13) www.theroot.com/articles/culture/2013/02/slavery in New York wall street was built with African help.html (How Slave Trade Made NY)
(14) Song of Solomon; Excerpt (pg. 9)
(15) John Newton, *Amazing Grace*, 1779 wikipedia.org 144-149
(16) http://time.com/3694053/veteran-suicide/

Pg. 2 (prosebeforehos.com) photo
Pg. 35 (Superiority Complex) http://www.merriam-webster.com/dictionary/superiority%20complex
Pg. 70 Inner Land, Eberhard Arnold Plough Publishing House

Broken Dreams image © by Lester Wingate
Poem The Middle Passage © by Lester Wingate
Hear Us © by Lester Wingate
In God We Trust © by Lester Wingate

Coming Soon: **"Can't Do No Wrong"**

www.ingramcontent.com/pod-product-compliance
Lightning Source LLC
Chambersburg PA
CBHW040321300426

44112CB00020B/2829